MONEY, BANKING, AND CREDIT

IN EASTERN EUROPE

GEORGE GARVY

FEDERAL RESERVE BANK OF NEW YORK

COPIES OF THIS BOOKLET are available from the Publications
Section, Federal Reserve Bank of New York, New York, N. Y.
10045, at   per copy. Educational institutions may obtain
quantities for classroom use at 65 cents per copy.

Library of Congress Catalog Card Number: 66-29107

Foreword

THIS booklet is another in the series published by the Federal Reserve Bank of New York to provide information that is not readily available on subjects not recently reviewed in economic literature. It also reflects the desire to make available to the public work done within the Federal Reserve Bank in the continuing study of banking practices and policies both here and abroad.

Mr. Garvy, who has visited most of the countries whose banking systems are here described, has had the benefit of many conversations with bankers, government officials, and economists in the countries of Eastern Europe.

Keynes once warned that money is a veil over the economy, obscuring the view for most people. On the other hand, the veil is probably not quite opaque and, to the extent that it clings to the object covered, the discerning observer can see at least the shape of the economy. This ought to be especially true when, as Mr. Garvy points out, the banking system is used to control the performance of the economy. Finally, at a time when the economies of these Eastern European countries seem to be in the course of a significant modification, the changes taking place in their banking systems illuminate the nature of the older forms and suggest the nature of the new.

ALFRED HAYES
President

New York City
September 1966

Acknowledgments

THE author owes a large debt of gratitude to banking officials of the countries covered by this study, who helped in assembling the underlying material and offered comments on the chapters dealing with their respective countries. Numerous associates at the Federal Reserve Bank of New York were helpful with comments and suggestions. The author has had the benefit of expert criticism and constructive suggestions from Professors Edward Ames, Purdue University; Gregory Grossman, University of California; Egon Neuberger, University of Michigan; and Raymond P. Powell, Yale University; as well as from Paul Gekker of the Division of International Finance at the Board of Governors of the Federal Reserve System and R. H. Gilchrist of the Overseas Department, Bank of England. Special thanks are due to Eugene Babitchev, Economist in the International Research Department of this Bank, for untiring research assistance and numerous suggestions. The readability and structure of the booklet were greatly improved by the perceptive editorial skill of Miss Elizabeth Todd. Miss Abigail M. Cantwell prepared the manuscript for publication and saw it through the final stages of editing and printing.

Contents:

Money, Banking, and Credit
in Eastern Europe

Introduction

The economic policies of the Soviet Union and the other communist countries of Eastern Europe have been undergoing important changes in recent years and are likely to have a significant effect on the role played by money, banking, and credit in those nations. But the ultimate shape of the evolving innovations is still far from clear. Some countries have been moving in the new direction more rapidly than others, and there are also considerable country-to-country differences in specific implementation. In all the countries under review it is possible to discern a shift toward decentralization of planning, reduction in the number of plan targets, and increased use of the market mechanism and the profit criterion, with greater reliance on financial incentives and "credit levers" for the "steering of the economy". At the same time the basic attributes of Soviet-type economies—state ownership of the means of production, central planning of economic activity, and the attendant financial structures, relationships, and processes—remain intact.

As this study will show, the monetary and credit systems of the communist countries differ fundamentally from the corresponding arrangements in the West. What is here referred to as the "standard" system, embodying the basic communist conceptions regarding the role of banks in the economy, was first given firm shape in the Soviet Union during the early 1930's and then introduced into

9

the other Eastern European countries after they came under communist control. Its outlines have not been significantly altered by the recent and impending modifications. Therefore Part I focuses on this standard system—the characteristics that are common to the countries under review—with only incidental references to national variations or evolving changes. The final chapter of Part I makes use of this essential background to describe and evaluate the more important of the changes now being introduced or experimented with. Concrete examples in Part I are given mainly for illustrative purposes. Thus, reference to a certain procedure being used, say, in Poland does not mean that it is not employed elsewhere. While in some instances all the countries in which a given procedure is practiced are mentioned, in certain other instances it could not be readily ascertained whether such procedures are in use in countries other than those indicated in the text and it was deemed not worthwhile to undertake the required research.

Part II, divided into separate chapters on the various countries, provides more detail on institutional and operational deviations from the prototype and on the specific nature of recent innovations. The chapters of Part II do not, however, attempt a detailed description for each country; even if this were possible with the available data, it would unduly extend the length of the study. Thus the Part II chapters are relatively short and by necessity uneven, with the larger and more industrialized countries receiving the more minute consideration.

The study is confined to seven countries, and it is these seven alone that are referred to in using the term Eastern European countries. In order of population size, they are the Soviet Union, Poland, Rumania, East Germany, Czechoslovakia, Hungary, and Bulgaria. Albania is omitted because of its relative economic insignificance and the dearth of accessible material, and Yugoslavia because it has been going its own way for over fifteen years, having gradually abandoned most of the specific characteristics of Soviet-type monetary and banking arrangements and blending the remainder with structural and policy elements taken from the West. Apart from Yugoslavia, however, the standard system described in Part I also applies, with only minor modifications, to the existing arrangements in the other communist countries not included in this study: Albania, China, North Korea, North Vietnam, Outer Mongolia, and even Cuba.

Although the Soviet Union was the prototype for the other Eastern European countries, its considerable differences from them should be kept in mind. Its population is more than double that of the other countries combined, and unlike the others its resources are so extensive and diversified as to provide the basis for relative economic self-sufficiency. Moreover, its economic system has evolved through a long succession of changes, going back to the chaotic conditions that resulted from the widespread destruction and disorganization following World War I and the years of civil war. In the other countries the new regimes shaped along Soviet lines were instituted against a different historical background and have been in existence for a much shorter period. Elements of the Western heritage have survived in these countries to a surprising degree, and there is widespread familiarity with the workings of a competitive market economy, whereas in the Soviet Union the pre-revolutionary past has become a dim memory.

This study, however, aims primarily at synthesis rather than contrast, and its analysis is neither comparative nor historical. Nor does it attempt an overall evaluation of the success of Eastern European monetary policy in achieving price stability. As is shown in Chapter 1, the pursuit of this goal—and of other economic goals, such as optimum allocation of resources and maximum efficiency in their use—entails a broad range of policies. Thus even with reference to a specific situation it would not be possible, without far more comprehensive analysis than is attempted here, to pinpoint the effectiveness of monetary policy as contrasted with other government policies—a difficulty, in fact, that is not unknown to analysts of Western economies.

An effort has been made to avoid semantic difficulties by giving preference to familiar terminology—for example by writing "deposits" where the official term is "remainders in current accounts". But deceptive similarities in terms—such as "acceptances"—are noted. In a few instances, Russian terms, which are employed in Eastern Europe and in Western specialized professional literature, are used to denote concepts that have no adequate counterpart in English. Except on matters of detail, which are annotated in text footnotes, published sources are listed in the bibliography that follows Part II.

PART I

1. Financial Characteristics of the Centrally Planned Economy

All the communist countries of Eastern Europe are now attempting, in various degrees, to make use of the market process. Many of the changes are being introduced only gradually, however, and in most countries details are still to be worked out for some of the most significant changes. In the meantime, the basic features of centrally planned economies remain intact. Production targets, formulated mainly in physical terms, are set by the central government and embodied in specific directives, usually cast in the form of output plans. Designated governmental agencies specify for each enterprise, or group of enterprises, the kinds and sources of inputs and the destination of outputs. Since all basic planning is in real magnitudes ("material balances"), the role of money is mainly to provide a common denominator (*numéraire*) for aggregation and projection. The allocation of resources is determined by the central plan and not through the price system. All prices are set by authority, and wage rates and total payroll costs of individual enterprises are strictly controlled. Consumer prices and transfer prices among producers are seldom changed, because stable prices facilitate global planning and an orderly distribution and redistribution of the national product. Administrative decisions, and not market adjustments, are relied upon to correct disequilibria and deviations from plans. Until experiments with more flexible policies were begun in recent years, individual enterprises in the government-owned sector of the economy (which, in each country, accounts for all but a small percentage of total output outside agriculture) had little scope for deciding between production alternatives or for making investment decisions.

THE CENTRAL ROLE OF THE BUDGET

All financial flows in the Eastern European countries, whether related to the movement of goods or to the flow of investment, are influenced by output plans and by direct controls over funds spent. They are not market determined and, indeed, there are no credit or capital markets. Instead the budget of the national government assumes the key role in the distribution of the national product. All major macroeconomic decisions — such as the division of current output between investment and consumption — are embodied in the government budget. In particular, the financial counterpart of the flow of real resources into investment is for the most part channeled through the budget. The national budget also fulfills an important allocative function with regard to investment flows (between industry and agriculture, among industries and regions), which in the free market economies is performed largely through the market process.

The budget is thus the most important funnel for all payments flows and the most important component of overall financial planning. Receipts of the state-owned enterprises in excess of expenditures for direct costs (mainly labor and materials) are siphoned off into the budget, either through taxes or by the transfer of profits (except for a relatively small part to be invested or spent for collective consumption by the enterprises themselves). About half of the national income of each country flows through the budget, a much larger proportion than in the United States and the other leading industrial countries of the West. This higher proportion results primarily from two facts: first, the channeling through the budget of the bulk of all investment (in working as well as fixed capital); and, second, the financing of a very large part of expenditures of all lower units of government through transfers from the national budget. Moreover, the bulk of "collective consumption" — which includes not only free educational, health, and other services, but also subsidies for housing, transportation, and the like — is budget financed.

Financing of investment in the government sector of the economy involves essentially transfers from the accounts of enterprises to the budget (and vice versa). Voluntary savings provide a very minor though growing counterpart of real investment. The, in effect, forced sale of government bonds to the population, resorted to in various communist countries in the first postwar years (in the Soviet Union until 1957-58), must be regarded as a measure for preserving monetary equilibrium by reducing consumption, rather than as a normal means of financing investment.

THE SEPARATION OF PAYMENTS FLOWS

A considerable part of the activity of the banking system centers on the administration of a two-circuit payments mechanism — cash and "noncash". Currency is used for virtually all payments between the government (including the state-owned enterprises) and the population (as wage earners but also as entrepreneurs, to the extent that farming and some other activities remain in private hands). Practically all consumer expenditures are made in currency. The flow of purchasing power to consumers is planned to match the available supply of goods and services, plus an estimated increase in cash balances (supported by an increase in currency in circulation). Savings accounts (and, in some cases, bonds issued by savings banks or by the government) and hoarding of currency are the only means open to the population for accumulating financial assets. In contrast, all payments among enterprises, organizations, and the government (except very small and strictly limited amounts) involve transfers on the books of the banking system; this noncash circuit is best thought of as the counterpart of check circulation in Western countries. The relationship between the two circuits, which correspond to separate markets for consumer goods and producer (including raw material and intermediary) goods, will be discussed in Chapter 3.

Separation of the two circuits not only facilitates control but also makes it easier to detect disequilibria, bottlenecks, and various shortfalls in the execution of economic plans. Because of the separation of the payments stream into two watertight compartments, and the considerable differences between the functions of balances in the two sectors, the concept of the total money supply has very limited analytical significance in the countries of Eastern Europe.

EQUILIBRIUM THROUGH PLANNING

Maintenance of equilibrium conditions and achievement of growth objectives are supposed to result from proper overall planning of material resources, and not through influencing, indirectly, aggregate pecuniary demand and its structure or the cost and availability of money and capital. From its very origin, Soviet financial planning has been "derivative" — based on material balances, in which specific kinds of physical resources are allocated to achieve growth under conditions of overall equilibrium. Monetary flows are planned as the counterpart of physical flows, and adjusted to changes in such flows. Equilibrium between supply and monetary demand for consumer goods and services is to be attained by production, price, and wage decisions taken by the planning authorities. Equilibrium in the cash circuit is achieved when wage and other payments to the population equal the monetary value of the consumer goods and services that are to be produced by the economy at established prices which, ideally, remain stable for relatively long periods of time. Adjustments needed to maintain such an equilibrium are taken by the planning, not by the monetary, authorities.

14

Planning for growth under conditions of overall equilibrium of monetary demand and supply takes the form of an interlocking system of financial plans. In effect, these plans are projections, in the form of balances, of sources and uses of funds in the various sectors of the economy. They vary in their makeup—some flows are on a gross, others on a net, basis and a few are drawn up in stock terms. Some are, in effect, detailed operating plans while others are more in the nature of broad guidelines for the use of policy-making bodies. There are also considerable differences among countries in the number and articulation of such plans and in the extent to which the plans represent merely internal working documents or approach the status of binding operational directives. Moreover, the role of financial planning itself has been undergoing important changes in recent years. All this is to be discussed in some detail in Chapter 4.

Whatever the official status of the monetary plans, actual performance measured against plan figures provides a day-to-day check on the working of the economy—indeed the only overall check. Monetary flows in the socialized sector, recorded through the banking system (by entries in the appropriate accounts), reveal deviations from planned real flows and thus mirror disequilibria and bottlenecks in the real processes. Money thus performs an important signal function, but it is not relied on to any significant degree as an adjuster. Remedial action normally comes through direct intervention by the authorities in charge of production and distribution ("the economic organs") and through fiscal and pricing policies and other tools intended to change output levels and patterns directly. Much of what appears to be monetary action is rather the exercise of administrative functions by the banking system in support of policies formulated elsewhere in the planning structure.

The control of individual enterprises is shared among national, regional, and local authorities. As a general rule, enterprises producing basic materials, capital goods, or consumption goods for the national market are subordinated to a ministry. The other enterprises, which tend to be smaller, are responsible to regional political entities (federated republics in the Soviet Union) or to municipalities (which typically have jurisdiction over such enterprises as local retail and service establishments, bakeries, utilities, or movie theatres). Several enterprises of national significance, or even all units in the same industry, are frequently joined for administrative purposes into organizations variously called trusts, combines, groups, firms, aggregations, associations, and the like. (For the sake of consistency, these will hereafter be uniformly referred to as associations; they are normally subordinated to a ministry in charge of a given group of industries.)

Because of the basic reliance on planning in terms of real flows, and the central importance of the national budget for financial planning, the functions of money and credit in Eastern Europe are radically different from the roles they play in free market economies. Ownership of money does not give an absolute command over resources. The individual can acquire only consumer goods and strictly limited categories of property for personal use. Small service establishments, artisans, and independent farmers also can acquire producer goods—and this is of some importance in countries like East Germany and Poland; but these nonsocialized sectors are not significant (with the major exception of agriculture in Poland). In the state sector, money may be used only in conformity with the plan; credit gives command over resources only if acquisition of the resources is foreseen in the plan, while plan allocation of resources carries with it an almost automatic claim on credit. The role of monetary flows is to implement the planners' intentions, not to invoke response or to correct movement away from equilibrium ("neutral money"). The power of money to influence real processes is severely limited by direct administrative controls. Attempts to use monetary incentives in order to guide economic activity have been made in recent years, but so far on a limited scale only, as discussed in Chapter 8.

The countries of Eastern Europe know no credit-granting institutions other than banks. To a very limited extent, banks have been used since the mid-1950's to finance certain minor kinds of fixed investment (as more fully discussed in Chapter 5), but the main role of credit under the standard system is to provide the bulk of the financing of inventories at the various levels of production and distribution. Consumer credit and financing of cooperative and individual home building have become important only in recent years. Where a significant part of agriculture remains in private hands, notably in Poland, some efforts have been made since the mid-1950's to provide credit to farmers, both for seasonal needs and for improving technology. Except in East Germany, Czechoslovakia, and Poland, practically no credit is available to private enterprise in the other sectors of the economy. Changes of a rather marginal nature in credit policy and techniques, intended to provide somewhat greater flexibility, were made in the Soviet Union after the death of Stalin in 1954; these were also copied in the other countries, although in some cases in a modified form, and some changes were introduced for which there was no Soviet example. Until very recent years, however, such divergences involved chiefly techniques and details, rather than a fundamental reappraisal of the potentialities of monetary and credit policy.

16

The aggregate volume of credit is determined almost automatically by the production and distribution goals set in real terms. The proper amount of total working capital and the extent to which it consists of the enterprises' own resources (designated as "own funds") are determined by the central authorities for each individual industry. Thus changes in the volume of credit are, for the most part, the counterpart of changes in the volume of inventories, unless planning authorities decide to change the relative share of enterprise funds and bank credit in the carrying of inventories. Under the standard system, as Chapter 5 will show, the granting of credit is almost automatic, once the borrower's output plan has been approved, and the mechanics of credit granting is geared to rigid rules. Changes in the cost and availability of credit are not relied on as the means of achieving changes in resource use, although in recent years differentiation in interest rates has been increasingly used to achieve greater efficiency and to favor socially desirable activities. The prevailing official view is that the essential function of the credit system is the redistribution of cash balances (temporarily redundant enterprise balances, budget surpluses, and consumer savings) rather than credit creation.

During the first twenty-five years after the credit reforms of 1930-32, the credit policy of the Soviet Union was concerned exclusively with providing the payments counterpart of the movement of real goods through the production and distribution process. The other countries originally copied the Soviet credit system to the smallest details. In very recent years, however, at least some of the countries have begun to explore the possibility of adapting credit administration techniques as instruments of active credit policy. Progress in this direction will be reviewed in the chapters devoted to the individual countries.

LIQUIDITY POSITION OF ENTERPRISES

Since the ability of enterprises to acquire goods depends, theoretically at least, on the planners' intent and not primarily on liquidity, the liquidity position of the enterprise sector is ostensibly of no concern to credit policy. In effect, however, administrative and financial controls have not proved sufficient to prevent "unplanned" spending: enterprises have frequently made use of their financial resources to support their operations, as dramatically evidenced in several instances of inflationary outbursts—especially in 1950-53—in all the smaller communist countries with the exception of East Germany. Thus, while the monetary system has no way of influencing the liquidity of the socialized sector on a day-to-day basis, some countries have at times resorted to the device of temporarily sterilizing (blocking) enterprise balances or imposing limitations on their use.

The individual enterprise, which under the standard system has very limited latitude in managing its working capital, is rarely confronted with liquidity problems in the same sense as firms in capitalist countries. Its liquidity position has no direct bearing on its fixed investment plans, since these are, with negligible exceptions, implemented by financing from budgetary resources. Loans are made automatically on bills of lading to cover the standard collection period, and usually provision is made for easy access to bank credit in order to finance unforeseen expenditures, such as bulges in inventories of raw materials due to deliveries ahead of or beyond schedule. At the same time, considerable emphasis is placed on "improving the payments discipline", since failure to pay on time is tantamount to extending interunit credit; it disrupts the circular flow of capital and creates payments difficulties all down the line.

While the management of an enterprise has usually little difficulty in temporarily replenishing working funds through bank loans, its ability to use its own bank balance is strictly circumscribed. In communist countries the absolute order to pay is unknown; all payments must be documented as consistent with the applicable plan, and the purpose of the payment is normally verifiable from the underlying documents. Interenterprise payments are usually made not by check but on the basis of drafts supported by documents related to the shipment of goods, and collection of payments for shipments (or services rendered) requires time-consuming movement of documents. Claims arising from production and distribution are nonnegotiable and nonassignable: they can give rise only to deposit transfers (settlements) between the accounts of the actual buyer and seller.

A shortage of funds normally results in difficulties of one sort or another, but the accumulation of free funds (excess liquidity in Western terms) confers little advantage, since it does not in itself entitle the enterprise to purchase additional resources. It may actually lead to a loss of working capital (if the superior economic authority directs the enterprise to relinquish the excess to other enterprises), or failure to obtain an additional allocation ("replenishment") of working capital from the budget next year, or even a permanent reduction of allotted working capital. Policy makers in communist economies have an interest in keeping the enterprises' own working funds at a minimum, so that extension of credit would give the bank a greater lever to exert tighter controls over each enterprise.

Indeed, the total volume of credit does not have the same significance that it has in the Western countries. The dividing line between credit and working capital owned by the individual enterprise is fluid and not of great significance in itself. The choice between more "own" capital and more credit hinges on overall policy considerations, embodied in industrywide "norms" (prescribed standard ratios). Since all capital in the state enterprise sector is owned by the government and is merely assigned to individual enterprises, a working-capital shortage in any given enterprise can be remedied either by granting it more credit or by adding to its capital (through budgetary resources or through transfers from other enterprises administered by the same ministry or from other "higher echelon" organizations in the economic administration). In principle, all state enterprises operate in part with borrowed funds, mainly because it is desired to increase control by the banking authorities, but the precise share of loans in working funds varies, in accordance with considerations discussed in Chapter 5.

THE ROLE OF THE BANKING SYSTEM

Even before he took power, Lenin envisaged the banking system as becoming the backbone of the socialist state's administrative apparatus. Nationalization of private banking and establishment of a government monopoly of all foreign exchange transactions were among the first economic measures taken by the Bolshevik government in 1917. In the other Eastern European countries, foreign exchange transactions were virtually a government monopoly at the time the communists obtained a dominant position, and nationalization of banks and other financial institutions was uniformly one of the first actions of the new governments. Centralization of bank credit appeared to be a logical concomitant of centralized planning and management of production and distribution.

The particular form of banking organization developed originally in the Soviet Union combines in the State Bank most of the attributes of a central bank with those functions of commercial banking that are relevant in the communist economy, and also with a wide range of activities related specifically to the characteristics of such economies. The term "monobank" fits well this type of banking institution. As will be described in the following chapter, the monobank is supplemented by a small number of banks that serve special functions, including an Investment Bank, which is a key institution for channeling funds into fixed capital.

In specific terms, the monobank is the *bank of issue* and is responsible for the regulation of note circulation. It manages the gold and foreign exchange reserves, in close cooperation with (and in some cases under the direction of) the Ministry of Finance and the Ministry of Foreign Trade (which in all countries of Eastern

Europe is responsible for administering the foreign trade monopoly). In most of the countries, as is more fully discussed in the next chapter, the financing of foreign trade, and even of related domestic activities, has in recent years been shifted to special foreign trade banks.

The monobank (along with the other banks, to the limited extent that they extend short-term credit) is the sole *source of short-term credit,* as the extension of direct interenterprise ("commercial") credit is forbidden. The bank is not the ultimate but the only lender. Since control of credit is exercised directly, the monobank is not concerned with the same problems (such as controlling the reserves or liquidity of independent commercial banks) or activities (such as discounting and open market operations) as central banks in Western countries. As there are no financial markets or instruments (except savings bonds held by individuals), authorities do not have to worry about the prices of financial assets.

The monobank services the *currency needs* of the entire economy, including the savings banks and all specialized banks, where these exist as separate entities. Its offices act as *agents for specialized banks* in localities where these are not represented.

Since all payments within the socialized sector are transfers on its books, the monobank is the one and all-encompassing *settlements and clearing center* of the country. It keeps the accounts of the national government and of all subordinate government units, and performs all the usual *fiscal agency functions* carried out by central banks in Western countries (e.g., the collection and disbursement of revenue to support regular government activities, the issue and redemption of public loans). Of the proceeds deposited at the monobank from the sale of goods by the state enterprises, a part is paid out in cash for wages and the remaining part is credited to various accounts through book transfers. Thus it functions as a *social accounting center,* which not only keeps track of payments flows but, in many cases, also allocates single payments among several special-purpose accounts.

Because payments flows are planned and tied to plan fulfillment, all such monobank operations as cash withdrawals, book transfers, and credit extensions involve an *audit function* to check conformity of payment to underlying authorization. This important activity—essential to what is called "control by the ruble" (or the forint, or the koruna), which is a basic feature of centrally planned economies—entails more than financial supervision; indeed, it makes the monobank a key part of the policy and administrative apparatus of the communist state.

In view of its manifold functions, it is logical that the monobank is an active participant in all phases of economic planning. It is also a major, and frequently the main, channel through which any failures in the meshing of gears come to the attention of the authorities. But the monobank raises the flag without cracking the whip; when the signals it transmits require corrective action, this is normally taken through policy measures that emanate from the higher authorities of the state.

The difference between the monobank and both the central and the commercial banks of capitalist countries is reflected in the structure of the balance sheet. The assets side of the monobank's balance sheet consists mainly of loans to the various segments of the economy (possibly including a small amount of housing loans to individuals), in addition to gold and foreign exchange; it contains no government or private securities. Among the monobank's liabilities (in addition to capital accounts and note liabilities) are the free balances of its clients—the counterpart of demand deposits in capitalist countries. These balances are owned mainly by economic or governmental units and, to a lesser extent, by cooperative farms and nonprofit organizations. The only counterpart of the interbank balances held by banks in Western countries is the uncommitted deposits of specialized banks. There are no time deposits and only a negligible amount of deposits of individuals.

The monobank's activities have some similarities to those of central banks in underdeveloped countries, with their rudimentary or nonexistent money and capital markets, their reliance on government for the bulk of capital formation, the relatively large volume of lending either by the central bank directly or through development banks, and largely fixed or stable rates of interest. Differences between Eastern Europe and the West in regard to the functions of money and credit and the central bank are considerable and basic, as will be shown in more detail in the following chapters.

SOURCES OF BANK FUNDS

No State Bank of any country of Eastern Europe currently publishes data on the liabilities side of its balance sheet. It is known, however, that funds available for lending are acquired each year from a combination of the following sources (disregarding any resources of foreign origin): cumulative budget surpluses of previous years (a main means of achieving equilibrium in the economy), an increase in capital resources (from profits or transfers from the budget), an increase in note circulation, funds held at the State Bank by the specialized banks,

21

reserves of social insurance funds (where they exist as separate entities, as in Czechoslovakia), deposits of savings banks (particularly where, as in the Soviet Union, they have no lending business of their own), and an increase in balances of enterprises and organizations. The last of these, being strictly controlled and kept at a minimum, is likely to be of greater significance from a seasonal than from a longer run point of view. In the Soviet Union, for instance, such balances at the beginning of 1965 stood at 12.1 billion rubles which, in relation to the value of industrial output, is considerably below the ratio between the level of commercial bank balances maintained by United States corporations and the value of the corporate product.

Even though the banking literature of the communist countries keeps repeating that the State Bank can make loans only within the limits of resources at its disposal, and though considerable day-by-day efforts are made to attract ("mobilize") additional resources (for instance, by inducing farm cooperatives to keep their free funds with banks), the implied analogy with commercial banks in capitalist countries is misleading. The State Bank cannot lose funds to any other bank, since it accounts for 95 per cent or more of total credit and is the depository of the uncommitted funds of all other banks. Issue of additional currency may be, and almost certainly will be, the result of any additional lending, but this merely represents a shift in the composition of the liabilities that match the loans added to the assets side of the balance sheet. The real, indeed the only, limit to the extension of bank credit in communist countries—where bank liabilities are not subject to reserve requirements and there is full administrative control of foreign payments—is determined by macroeconomic decisions made by the political and planning authorities and embodied in the financial plans.

THE BANK AND ITS CLIENTELE

The relationship between the monobank and its clientele also bears little resemblance to the corresponding relationship in capitalist countries. Rather than being an agent of the depositor, the monobank, when dealing with the individual enterprise, is, in fact, the representative of the state; the population at large has no direct contact with it. It protects the interests of the state by debiting from the depositor's account—in most cases, automatically—the various payments due the Treasury. If necessary, it extends credit to meet such payments. More generally, criteria that the bank applies in relations with its clientele are tied to the borrower's execution of the economic plan, to which the meeting of the

22

borrower's financial obligations to the bank is subordinated. Each enterprise, unit of government, or nonprofit (voluntary) organization has to bank with the single office in whose territory it is located. This arrangement obviously provides no incentive for the management and personnel of any unit of the banking system to improve service in order to retain or attract depositors.

Until the emergence of new trends in recent years, the bank and its customers were merely involved in a web of impersonal accounting relationships, embracing set, uniform, and rigid rules, few alternatives, a minimum of flexibility, and supervision that reached into the minute details of an enterprise's activities and amounted in effect to a continuous and detailed audit of physical and financial performance. The monobank used no other criterion for measuring performance than the degree of success with which an enterprise discharged its current financial obligations (maintained a sufficient balance to pay bills and loans when due) and avoided exceeding norms—most importantly, the inventory norms—imposed from the outside by planning authorities and various economic administrations, including ministries.[1]

MONETARY POLICY IN A PLANNED ECONOMY

From the foregoing brief summary it is clear that the functions of monetary policy in planned economies are very different from those it serves in the West. In the communist countries, as elsewhere, the basic objective of economic policy is to achieve optimum growth rates without exposing the existing price structure to pressures caused by imbalances between the flow of consumer purchasing power and the availability of consumer goods. And the underlying analysis of capabilities—in terms of available real resources—and of the required changes in money supply, credit, and financial flows resulted in procedures not much different from those used in making macroeconomic projections in Western countries. But in formulating and implementing monetary policies that will serve their objectives, the two types of economies differ completely, reflecting their fundamental differences in capital ownership, economic organization, and political and social philosophy.

---

[1] *See Robert W. Campbell,* Accounting in Soviet Planning and Management *(Cambridge, Massachusetts: Harvard University Press, 1963), pages 205 ff.*

In Western countries the formulation of monetary policy is a continuous process, responding flexibly to changes in the performance of the market economy. In communist countries, monetary policy is embodied in all-embracing financial plans, which carry final authority and are changed only at fixed intervals. Although one can identify the nature of credit and note issue policies pursued by a communist country, and show what policies it follows with regard to encouraging personal saving, providing financing for small-scale capital improvements, or managing foreign exchange reserves, it is difficult to tie these separate aspects into something that would add up to a socialist monetary policy. But in all such matters the banking system acts merely as a vehicle for the execution of broader government decisions as embodied in the detailed plans; monetary action is not geared to the market but is determined by administrative processes centered on the planned allocation of resources. The familiar tools of monetary policy available to Western central banks are irrelevant. In communist countries, monetary policy is concerned primarily with assuring the efficiency of currency circulation and of the payments mechanism and with facilitating the economic performance of enterprises, while fiscal policy is heavily relied upon to assure balance between aggregate demand and supply.

In fact, one would look in vain in the writings of Soviet economists, who so far have been setting the tone in the other countries of Eastern Europe as well, for an explicit discussion of monetary policy. Typically, Soviet textbooks and treatises merely discuss the various functions of credit in the socialist economy. The more sophisticated treatment makes a distinction between the "functions" and the "role" of credit, reserving the first term for the place of credit in the socialist economy and equating "role" with the results achieved in accelerating growth and output.[2] Economic literature in Eastern Europe deals with the practical problems of controlling monetary circulation, crediting production and trade, and financing capital investment, usually under separate headings, but it does not discuss monetary policy, as such, or its relationship to fiscal policy, even though in the communist countries the two are closely integrated and the relationship between the monobank and the Ministry of Finance is at least as close as between central bank and government in Western countries. Similarly, banking

---

[2] See, for instance, Iu. E. Shenger, Ocherki sovetskogo kredita (Essays on Soviet Credit), Moscow, 1961, pages 63-64.

officials, in their published speeches and articles, typically focus on how the State Bank can best implement the economic plan or party decisions. Such statements clearly reflect the implementary nature of the monobank's activities and characteristically treat the monetary aspects of those activities (credit, currency circulation) on the same footing as routine operations (mutual offsets) or control functions (control over payroll disbursements).[3]

Even though the monobank plays essentially the role of an implementing agency, it has significant functions in the central administration's efforts to influence aggregate demand and stimulate growth. It contributes—to an extent that varies from country to country—to the determination of realistic plan targets and of the proper magnitudes that will "correctly" implement them, as well as serving indispensably in furthering the proper execution of the various financial plans. The monobank's role in economic administration is enhanced by an organizational advantage: in contrast to the various ministries, organized on an industry principle, and to regional economic bodies, it has a close and continuous contact, not only with specific branches or areas, but with the entire economy.

Nevertheless, the fact remains that, when the level and distribution of spending power do not conform with the underlying plan, the means used to correct the disequilibria are not changes in the cost and availability of credit but administrative improvisation by the monobank—unless the matter is so serious that higher echelon government or party authorities step in with a change in the ground rules. The monobank is an adjuster, not a steerer; its role—to borrow Robert V. Roosa's terminology, coined in a different context—is defensive rather than dynamic.

Communist countries have no effective means of controlling the excess liquidity of the population sector and its threat to price stability, except through the harsh and dramatic measures of currency conversions and upward price adjust-

---

[3] *In the authoritative Soviet two-volume* Dictionary of Finance and Credit *(issued by the official publishing house specializing in financial literature), there is no entry for "monetary policy". "Credit policy" is defined as "a system of measures in the area of credit, designed to secure the economic interests of the ruling class". There is no definition for a socialist economy, but a short review of the tasks of credit policy is prefaced by the statement that "In the Soviet Union credit policy corresponds to the tasks that the government places before the country in each phase of the construction of socialism and communism" (Vol. I, pages 584-85). "Credit restrictions" (page 585) are described as "limitations or reductions in the volume of credit, which are put into effect by capitalist banks and the bourgeois state", and correspondingly, "credit expansion" (page 591) is "enlargement of credit, put into effect by capitalist banks and the bourgeois state, which exceeds the growth of production, stimulates overproduction and the coming about of economic crises". There is no reference to a possible role of either process in a socialist economy.*

ments (and in some cases, until the mid-1950's, through forced loans placed with the population).[4] Thus a primary objective of financial planning and action is to prevent excess liquidity of consumers from coming into existence and in general to avoid inflation, both overt and repressed (though the word "inflation" is banned from the vocabulary of Soviet economists, at least in relation to their own economy). Nevertheless, inflationary pressures have recurrently arisen in all the countries of Eastern Europe. To combat inflationary tendencies, to remove their causes, and to re-create conditions favorable to maintenance of price stability, centrally planned economies rely on a combination of fiscal, price, wage, foreign trade, and monetary and credit measures, and also on administrative shifts in the allocation of resources (and, if necessary, changes in planned targets).[5]

The nature of the monobank's role in monetary policy has been clearly stated in an interview given by Dr. O. Pohl, General Director of the State Bank of Czechoslovakia: "Of decisive importance for the expansion of an active financial policy is a structurally sound and well-balanced plan. Once the material resources have been incorrectly employed, the bank will be too late with whatever measures it could take." Increased bank participation in the preparation and drawing-up of the plan is desirable, he said, "to enable the bank to step in with its own knowledge and demands when there is still time to influence the anticipated employment of material means, in other words to strengthen the preventive character of the bank's role".[6] After the plan is accepted, the monobank's efforts are directed toward keeping the monetary variables in line with the projections that relate changes in credit and currency circulation to real targets. Within the

---

[4] *The experience of currency conversion, common to all these countries in the first postwar years, left few fond memories, though the 1947 conversion in the Soviet Union, and some others, did produce a more favorable ratio of exchange for small savings and for certain groups of account holders. See E. Ames, "Soviet Bloc Currency Conversions",* American Economic Review, *June 1954.*

[5] *Even a cursory review of the Eastern European countries' efforts to neutralize the inflationary overhang of World War II and to combat the subsequent succession of inflationary threats would exceed the limits of the study. Fortunately, adequate accounts of these developments are readily available. See John M. Montias, "Inflation and Growth: The Experience of Eastern Europe", in W. Baer and I. Kerstenetzky, Inflation and Growth in Latin America (Homewood, Illinois: Richard D. Irwin, 1964), pages 216-50; also F. Holzman, "Soviet Inflationary Pressures, 1928-50: Causes and Cures", Quarterly Journal of Economics, May 1960. For an (unorthodox) communist view of this problem, see B. Oyrzanowski, "Problems of Inflation under Socialism", in Inflation, Proceedings of a Conference held by the International Economic Association, edited by D. C. Hague (New York: St. Martin's Press, Inc., 1962), pages 323-58, and the several papers by Oyrzanowski and other Polish authors cited by Michael Kaser in his comments on the Montias article quoted above, pages 276-83.*

[6] Rudé Právo *(Prague), May 20, 1964.*

framework of the plan, credit policy can help bring about a more efficient use of the resources than the plan provides, and thus contribute to lowering costs. But the monobank will automatically validate any of the plan's misjudgments and shortcomings that are binding for it. And although it is expected to prevent spending in excess of stipulated amounts—particularly for wage disbursements and inventory building—it can do little to bring inadequate spending to target levels.

TOWARD GREATER RELIANCE ON "ECONOMIC LEVERS"

With the new policies that began to emerge in the post-Stalin era but which became generally accepted throughout Eastern Europe only by 1965, the role of the banking system has begun to change. In general, the new developments involve a downgrading of physical indicators and an elevation of profitability to a position as an indicator of success — in other words, a differentiation between good and poor performers, a more liberal treatment of the former, increased stress on financial performance, as compared with physical output, and greater reliance on initiative and on material incentives. Although the new policies that have been taking shape in recent years give greater latitude to the local bank official, they by no means change his position as agent of the state: the difference lies in a shift from the state's exclusive reliance on administrative controls to a system that makes increasing room for "steering by self-regulation", in which "economic levers" are assigned an active role.

The degrees to which the individual countries have at this writing moved away from the Soviet prototype vary greatly. It is clear that much greater variety in institutional arrangements and policies is developing as each country's specific conditions and experience, as well as the differing views on the way in which a communist economy can make use of the market mechanism and dispense with detailed administrative controls, are gradually being embodied in new banking legislation and regulations. It appears that any further moves in individual countries toward greater reliance on the impersonal mechanism of the market for achieving a more rational and more effective allocation of resources and greater efficiency in their use will be accompanied quite generally by an increased role assigned to financial criteria (including profits) and incentives. Credit policy is likely to play a greater and, in some respects, different role, losing much of its purely implementary character. In this process the bank official will become less concerned with the interpretation of regulations and gauging plan performance and more with evaluating the profitability of alternative uses of credit.

2. The Structure of the Banking System

In each country of Eastern Europe the banking structure was reshaped radically, soon after its communist party achieved complete control, along the lines of the system as it functioned in the Soviet Union at the outbreak of World War II. The Soviet system was copied in considerable detail: its structure and its basic principles of credit and monetary circulation, credit instruments and clearing arrangements, and later monetary and credit planning. Advisers from the Soviet Union were brought in, and standard Russian treatises and handbooks on money and banking were quickly translated. The only country in which imitation was delayed and not completed was East Germany; its banking system shows some interesting deviations from the Soviet prototype, made necessary by a number of factors, including the survival of remnants of a private sector more important in the economy than the vestiges of private enterprise in the other countries of Eastern Europe. Subsequently, East Germany was the first to proceed to a radical reorganization of its monobank, but in all other countries as well, after an initial period of imitation, banking and credit arrangements began to reflect in various degrees the specific needs of the country, and the Soviet prototype began to be modified.

CREATION OF THE COMMUNIST BANKING STRUCTURE

The banking systems of the Eastern European countries outside the Soviet Union were in varying stages of development before World War II. They followed the continental European pattern: there was a central bank and a small number of large banks, which had sizable direct investments in industry. In the more developed countries (Germany and Czechoslovakia) there were specialized credit institutions, particularly for agriculture, and various cooperative banks were active. The banks of the less developed countries were in part owned by foreign capital. In some of the countries the banking system underwent considerable changes during the war and even before it. That of Czechoslovakia was completely disorganized as a result of German occupation, and in other parts of Eastern Europe, notably in Poland, the territorial changes imposed by Hitler's Germany, and also German operations to finance the war, were reflected in changes in bank ownership and structure.

In each country the nationalization of the entire commercial banking system was one of the first steps toward the communist party's assumption of control over the private economy and its seizure of full political control. Subsequently, all commercial banks were liquidated or merged with the central bank into a single institution. Savings banks and other credit institutions, such as farm credit cooperatives, were reorganized, merged, and integrated into the new structure, or were liquidated.

The Soviet Union emerged from World War II with a banking structure which, after a quarter of a century of vicissitudes and reorganization, had reached a certain degree of stability, its place within the organizational framework of a centrally planned economy fairly well settled and defined. From the time of its establishment in 1921, the State Bank of the Soviet Union (Gosbank) had had the main attributes of a central bank; and as a result of the credit reforms of 1930-32 it had acquired the monopoly of short-term lending (enforced by the prohibition of direct financing of enterprises by customers, suppliers, or parent organizations). The many changes in the policies and organization of the Gosbank prior to the end of World War II cannot be discussed here in detail. By the time it was cast in the role of serving as the prototype for all countries of the world in which communist parties became the dominant power, only a few basic problems of organization remained controversial, such as the issue of whether specialized institutions should be organized along economic sectors (agriculture, construction) or by type of credit (long term versus short term). Coincidentally, the principles and procedures of credit policy had attained the status of rigid doctrine.

While some reassignments of specific responsibilities in the credit field have occurred in all countries of Eastern Europe, the basic structure is fairly similar since the original banking systems were replicas of Soviet institutions. Typically it involves the following institutions: the State Bank (monobank); the Investment Bank and other specialized banks, usually for the financing of agriculture and foreign trade and, in some countries, for facilitating and attracting private foreign exchange remittances from abroad; a national network of savings banks; and cooperative banks to finance artisan production and the other surviving forms of private enterprise. Broadly speaking all the banks other than the State Bank perform essentially only technical tasks and act as a kind of transmission belt between the monobank and the rest of the economy. The specific banking institutions operating in each country are described in Part II. The purpose of this chapter is to bring out common features and underlying principles, and to indicate recent trends to the extent that they represent a general reorientation of policies.

The State Bank (its precise name in the different countries is given in the individual chapters of Part II) is the keystone of the entire banking structure in each communist country. As a rule it is, or was until recently, under the supervision of the Ministry of Finance, with its head holding a position equivalent to that of a Deputy Minister of Finance. In some cases, the seal of government approval, which is carried by most financial plans established by the bank, has meant in practice approval by the Ministry of Finance.

In recent years there has been a tendency to de-emphasize the dependent status of the State Bank—the problem of the precise nature of the relationship between the central bank and the Ministry of Finance (or the Treasury) being not limited to communist countries. Thus the State Bank of the Soviet Union, which between 1946 and 1954 was formally under the Ministry of Finance, is now directly responsible to the Council of Ministers. And in several other cases (as in Czechoslovakia and Rumania) the head of the bank has been advanced in recent years, from a status equivalent of Deputy Minister of Finance, to ministerial rank (held by the head of the Gosbank since 1946), which may or may not carry with it attendance at cabinet meetings. The relationship between the State Bank and the Ministry of Finance is so close, however, that it is not deemed necessary to have a representative of the Ministry on the board of directors of the bank; indeed, the reverse is rather the rule, with the head of the State Bank participating in the highest policy group of the Ministry (such as the Collegium of the Ministry of Finance in Hungary and East Germany).

The State Bank has a close relationship also with many other parts of government, such as industrial ministries and the Planning Board, which coordinates financial and physical plans. Bank representatives participate in all major economic policy discussions and in the work of such policy-making bodies as price-setting boards.

Except as a collector of government revenue, the State Bank has few direct contacts with the population. It maintains only three broad types of accounts: those for economic units (whose activities involve cost accounting, or *khozraschet,* a Russian term used in most communist countries); those for the government; and those for cooperative and nonprofit organizations (both voluntary and budgetary). In countries where private business is of some significance and involves units larger than small trade establishments and repair and service shops, firms employing more than a certain number of workers and farmers owning more than a stipulated amount of land (in East Germany, for example, twenty hectares, which amounts to almost fifty acres) are required to keep their accounts with the State Bank. This arrangement gives the authorities an immediate and complete knowledge of their receipts and payments. Farm cooperatives usually have a choice between keeping their free funds at the State Bank, at the savings banks, or in currency. The number of accounts carried by the State Bank reflects the specific organization of the economy and the degree to which individual depositors are required to maintain separate accounts, such as loan accounts or accounts for depreciation reserves.

Because of the arrangements described in the next chapter, the State Bank's currency operations are very extensive, making it necessary to have cashier's windows throughout the country. These extensive cash operations, and also the function of maintaining a payments transfer mechanism, require a widespread network of branch offices in addition to the bank's large head office. Another important activity of the bank, in terms of the sheer volume of transactions involved, is the collection and disbursement of government revenue ("cash execution of the budget", in the terminology used in Eastern Europe): any separate Treasury collection and payments offices that originally existed in the various countries were absorbed by the State Bank.[1]

CONTROL FUNCTION OF THE STATE BANK

The manifold activities and responsibilities of the State Bank will become clear in the following chapters, but its control function—exercised on behalf of the government authorities in charge of the economy—requires special consideration here as background for the subsequent discussions. This function, which applies both to loans and to payments from bank balances, is essentially administrative in nature. It recalls the key role that Lenin assigned to the banking system in the communist state. Writing on the eve of the Bolshevik revolution, he stated in 1917:[2]

---

[1] *In the Soviet Union, for instance, the collection of all government revenue and its disbursement were gradually transferred to the Gosbank, beginning in 1925, when separate local offices of the Ministry of Finance were abolished; since 1948 the Gosbank has carried out this activity under a separate Department for the Cash Execution of the Budget, which has a counterpart in the State Banks of the other countries. The accounts of all local governments, too, were transferred in 1948 to the Gosbank, which now takes care of the operations of all levels of government.*

[2] *For a slightly different translation, see V. I. Lenin,* Collected Works *(London: Lawrence & Wishart, 1964), Vol. 26, page 106.*

Without big banks socialism could not be erected. The big banks are the "state apparatus" which we need to bring about socialism, and which we take ready-made from capitalism; our task here is merely to lop off what under capitalism mutilates this excellent apparatus, to make it even bigger. . . . A single giant State Bank, with branches in every rural district, in every factory, will constitute as much as nine tenths of the socialist administrative apparatus. This will be country-wide bookkeeping, country-wide accounting of the production and distribution of goods, this will be, so to speak, something in the nature of the skeleton of socialist society.

In its scope and meaning, the control exercised by the State Bank has no counterpart in Western banking. It can be understood only in the context of the centralized character of the communist state, the central role played by the government and the communist party in directing economic activities, and the insistence on compliance with plans. In the centrally planned economy, a "control organ" performs a variety of functions, which in our terminology range from audit and verification to day-to-day supervision with powers of enforcement. When sanctions available to the bank itself (see Chapter 5) prove inadequate to improve the financial management of an enterprise, the bank may have recourse to intervention by other government or party authorities. Thus in Hungary it may request the Ministry of Finance to appoint a financial trustee ("comptroller") for an enterprise, without whose approval no payment may be made.[3]

In the Eastern European countries the authority of government and that of the dominating communist party are intertwined. With few exceptions, all major economic decisions, including those in the field of credit and banking, are originally embodied in resolutions of party organs, and the specifics are spelled out in government decrees. This is true even in countries where the fiction is maintained that other parties (as in Czechoslovakia) or individuals without party affiliation (as in Hungary) participate in the government. Similarly, controls exercised by the State Bank are exercised on behalf of both the government and the party, and bank officials report to both, on the local as well as on the national level.

The banking system is used to make certain that the flows of funds through individual enterprises (and superior economic units) serve to implement the

---

[3] *I. Felvideki and R. Roka, "Crediting and Credit Planning in the Hungarian People's Republic", Den'gi i Kredit (hereafter D. K.), April 1964, page 85.*

economic plan. Bank control over such flows has thus a much broader purpose than to assure repayment of loans on schedule or prompt payment of taxes and profits into the budget. It is facilitated by a complex system of subaccounts aiming at a separation of circulating capital from amortization and other capital-account payments.

"Control by the ruble" involves practically all agencies of the economy, starting from an individual enterprise. To the important extent that it is exercised by the monobank, it means the monitoring of a performance that monetary action as such is not relied upon to influence. The monobank is involved in this function because it is the country's single centralized accounting center, its books reflecting the day-to-day performance of the economy as payments and currency flows are recorded. In a centrally planned economy, in which lines of authority are complex and confused and in which information flows through multilevel administrative channels and is registered on a multiplicity of badly coordinated indicators, the monobank is in a singularly advantageous position: changes in production and distribution as measured by one common denominator—money—are almost instantly reflected in great detail on its books. Its control functions are as important for the successful fulfillment of economic targets as its credit function.

Participation in "control by the ruble" is regarded as a natural extension of the activities of the banks. This control, however, has little in common with that exercised by monetary authorities in the Western countries. Its purpose is not to adjust the level or direction of monetary flows in order to achieve appropriate results in economic activity, but merely to make sure that the funds collected, spent, or borrowed coincide with the figures appearing in the applicable financial plan. Since all financial planning represents a translation of material targets into monetary terms, it is simply assumed that fulfilling financial plans on target is identical with achievement of the material goals.

Controls exercised by the monobank have a very broad scope, going far beyond matters involving the borrower-lender relationship. One of the main responsibilities of the bank is to enforce the "financial discipline" of all enterprises in the state sector, making sure that they meet their financial obligations to the bank and keep all expenditures within limits set by the plan. In fact, an important reason why the "own" working capital of economic units is kept low is that they are thereby forced to borrow, and thus afford the monobank a better opportunity for influencing directly their day-to-day activities.

The strategic position of the monobank is enhanced by the fact that under the extreme form of centralized controls—still in force in the Soviet Union but relaxed, to varying degrees, in the other countries—an enterprise (or any other economic unit) can use its "own" funds and the proceeds of loans only for specific purposes as detailed in the plan. The bank's execution of payment orders, whatever their purpose, involves pre-auditing, and in some cases post-auditing. Withdrawals of currency from any subaccount must be substantiated by documents specifying their purpose, and can be made only in conformity with stipulated rules, strict adherence to which is enforced by the bank. The monobank also makes sure that required payments, such as those for taxes or loan repayments, are made when due—a control that it exercises even over accounts maintained with it voluntarily, such as those of collective farms in the Soviet Union and in some other countries. Indeed, the entire payments system is used to enforce contracts between economic units and prompt fulfillment of all obligations toward the state budget.

Perhaps the most important area of control entails cash withdrawals for the payment of wages. The payroll account, or "wages fund", of each enterprise is programmed in great detail, but actual disbursements are contingent on the fulfillment of production goals. Overfulfillment—if it is deemed desirable in a given case—normally entitles the enterprise to withdrawals in excess of plan, in amounts that are linked by a fixed schedule to the extent of overfulfillment. This arrangement gives the monobank access to a broad range of production and cost data, inasmuch as unit cost is an element that is taken into account in establishing the eligibility of the enterprise to obtain additional payroll funds. Control over disbursements from the wages funds is usually very elaborate (except in Hungary where it has been practically given up), as it is intended to keep labor costs down and to prevent a "wage drift". In the Soviet Union, for instance, the Gosbank office prepares a calendar of disbursements for each enterprise, organization, and government unit it services, makes daily comparisons of actual and planned disbursements, and submits periodic reports to local and regional and party officials on the fulfillment of the wages fund plan.

Thus the control function goes beyond mere verification and may involve payments from and transfers between a depositor's separate accounts without his order, approval, or even knowledge, when the bank acts to protect the interests of the state (as for collection of taxes or other payments into the budget) or automatically applies certain rules and regulations pertaining to payments. Indeed, in some respects control amounts to the assumption of managerial responsibility —with State Bank officials deemed to be a better guardian of the state's interest than the state-appointed manager of the state enterprise. This situation has been

34

described as follows by a local official of the Gosbank:[4]

> Analysis of the activities of an individual enterprise in the fields of production and finance is undertaken not so much by its own staff, or the administrative agency to which it reports, or the sovnarkhoz [regional economic administration, since abolished], but by financial and banking officials. They visit the enterprises in order to uncover internal reserves [a Soviet euphemism for inefficiency], to develop concrete proposals for improvements, and to insist on their implementation.

Another official of the Gosbank outlined the activities of his branch office as follows:[5]

> The staff of the office takes an active part in the preparation of plans for merchandise turnover, territorial distribution of consumer goods, and the organization of trade; it has established control over the assortment and quality of consumer goods, and strives to restrict production of items for which there is no demand, to apply credit sanctions against trade organizations that do not achieve planned merchandise turnover or accumulate excessive inventories, and to ferret out local raw material resources and usable remnants for increasing the output of consumer goods. The office also works toward increasing the volume of services available to consumers, and it controls disbursements from the wages funds.

Some of the control activities of the State Bank (and of the other banking institutions) involve continuous checking of actual performance, as reflected by the bank's records, against the financial plans of the individual enterprises and the budgets of the various units of government. Others require on-the-spot inspection of inventories or accounting records. In some countries, including the Soviet Union, auditors of the State Bank are actually located in the large enterprises; in most countries, supervision is exercised through periodic visits by bank personnel.

The State Bank is not the only agency that exercises financial control functions. As a rule the financial records of an enterprise are subject to multiple audits, conducted by various ministries and government agencies on various administrative levels as well as by the monobank. These are not only burdensome and time consuming, but also result in overlapping responsibilites, without necessarily raising the quality of audits to adequate levels,[6] and there have recently been

---

[4] Ekonomicheskaia Gazeta (*hereafter* E. G.), *December 4, 1961.*

[5] *"Conferences and Seminars", D. K., June 1962, page 92.*

[6] *See, for instance, the article "30,000 Auditors", E. G., No. 48 (November 25, 1964), page 10.*

numerous complaints about them in the press of the Soviet Union. More significantly, there even seem to be some second thoughts on the deep involvement of monobanks in various control functions. Thus a leading authority, Professor V. Gerashchenko, a former official of the Gosbank who holds the chair of monetary circulation and credit at the Moscow Financial Institute, has written recently in the monthly review of that bank:[7]

> As is well-known, the basic task of banks in the socialist society is to engage in credit operations. The control functions, while important, must nevertheless be considered a secondary function of the banking apparatus.

In some of the countries the monobank is entrusted with specific control and reporting responsibilities that have only a remote relationship to banking functions. Thus in the Soviet Union the responsibility for reporting on the execution of production and labor utilization plans of individual enterprises has been transferred from the Central Statistical Administration to the Gosbank. In other countries the State Bank performs the accounting and reporting functions of individual economic units. In Rumania, for example, the monobank was charged with maintaining the accounting records of cooperative farms, in order to improve their financial performance; to fulfill this assignment it had to acquire a large staff of accountants to be attached to individual farm cooperatives.

The recent turn has been toward policies that would provide sufficient inducements and rewards to achieve results hitherto sought through a combination of administrative pressures, exhortation, and punishment, but it is not yet clear to what extent the elaborate mechanism of financial controls is to be dismantled.

STRUCTURE OF THE STATE BANK

The organizational structure of the State Bank also reflects the centralized nature of the planned economy. A strong headquarters organization is the apogee of a network of local offices numerous enough to bring bank officials into intimate contact with all state enterprises (including state farms), cooperative farms, and municipalities, with regional offices interposed between the head office and the local offices. All policies originate in the head office and are uniformly applied

---

[7] *"The Progressive Method of Crediting"*, D. K., *October 1965, page 14.*

throughout the national territory. Local offices merely apply regulations and directives issued at the center, and make loans and issue currency within the overall and specific quotas assigned to them. Uniformity of practices and (normally) daily reporting of transactions (along with periodic auditing by head office inspectors) assure that the center has complete knowledge of all operations.

Since all activities of the State Bank, and in particular its lending activities, are directly and closely related to the administrative organization of the socialized sectors of the economy, any change in that organization requires a corresponding change in the internal structure of the State Bank. Such organizational changes inevitably involve regroupment of industries or a shift of emphasis from the industry to the territorial principle and vice versa. Thus changes initiated in 1963 in the administration of the economy of East Germany led immediately to a restructuring of the State Bank. And the reorganization of Czechoslovakia's economy, decided upon in March of 1965 and effective at the start of 1966, has been accompanied by an internal reorganization of the State Bank of Czechoslovakia. The return to the industry principle in the Soviet Union is currently being accompanied by a corresponding reorganization within the Gosbank.

The key policy group of the State Bank is its board of directors (Managing Board), which consists exclusively of executive personnel and is usually appointed by the Council of Ministers. It typically includes the head of the bank, one or several of his deputies, and the heads of the most important departments. Only Poland has, besides the board of directors, a council representing a cross section of economic administrations and large enterprises, but this council meets infrequently. The Managing Board normally meets at least once a week, with the participation, if desirable, of senior officials.

The head of the State Bank is appointed by the supreme political authority of the country. Usually he is appointed from outside and not on the basis of extensive banking experience. In the Soviet Union the appointments have come typically from the senior staff of the Ministry of Finance, but in the other countries the individual named is, more frequently than not, a person in the administrative-political apparatus of the communist party, without previous banking experience. After doing a tour of duty with the bank, he may be assigned in a few years to a position quite unrelated to banking. Thus one should not be surprised to find as the chief executive officer of a State Bank a former general secretary of the Academy of Science or Deputy Minister of Finance. Similarly, a former president of the State Bank may become a member of the cabinet or an ambassador.

In recent years there has been a tendency to stress the central banking character of the State Banks by making changes in their names and in the titles of their heads. Thus the State Bank of Rumania has reverted to the prewar name National Bank, and its chief executive officer has assumed the title of Governor, instead of his former designation as Chairman of the Board, borrowed from the Soviet Union.

As regards its internal structure, the head office usually has five types of departments: first, policy departments, concerned with such matters as credit and foreign exchange planning and research; second, credit departments, usually articulated to correspond to the administrative structure of the economy, each division supervising all extension of credit to a given economic sector or territory; third, operating departments (cash, settlements, and fiscal agency functions); fourth, control departments (control of the wages fund and of borrowers, and internal auditing); and fifth, staff departments (personnel, legal, building operations, and so on).

Regional offices are staff organizations with few operating responsibilities, supervising a group of local offices and serving as a two-way link between them and the head office. A regional office normally has the following responsibilities. First, it supervises local offices and issues authorizations for specific actions (currency issue, transfer of unused lending authority to different loan categories or offices). Second, it fits together loan projections (requests) and, where credit planning has grass-roots elements, transmits them to the head office or, where planning is still from the top down, undertakes territorial breakdowns of national plans. Third, it deals with the needs of units that are administered by local and regional rather than national economic authorities. Fourth, it signals to the main office any "deviations from plan" or any other discrepancies between provision and the actual course of events that may require remedial action. And, finally, it makes sure that uniform policies reach into the remotest areas.

Much of the planning work and economic analysis is centralized in the regional offices, though the local offices—being in immediate contact with enterprises and cooperative farms—are the source of much of the specific knowledge underlying overall credit planning and administration. To the extent that greater flexibility in credit policy has developed in recent years, regional offices implement such changes; for instance, they may be made responsible for allocating unused credit lines (quotas) among local offices.

While a single tier of regional offices is typical, specific political conditions may introduce variations in some cases. Thus in Czechoslovakia the regional office in Bratislava is more important than the others, since it is the central office for the entire semiautonomous Slovakia. In the Soviet Union there is a "principal office" in the capital of each of the fifteen constituent republics, and there are several within the territory of the largest of the republics, the Russian Federation; each principal office supervises several regional offices. Principal offices are concerned only with industries and services of national significance, in contrast to the regional and local offices, which deal with credit problems of industrial and service establishments of strictly regional or local importance.

Local branches, being mainly operating offices, consist basically of three divisions—loans, cash, and settlements. They normally service all enterprises, cooperative farms, and governmental units located in their territory, which generally coincides with one or several lower administrative units of the country. In most cases the number of accounts serviced by a local office is small enough to enable bank officials to have intimate knowledge about each of them; where an office services a large or highly industrialized area, close contacts are assured by assigning groups of accounts to individual officials. Local offices usually bear the brunt of the control activities discussed above and of improving the flow of consumer goods and services—an activity that usually goes under the name of "mobilizing local resources". Although their managers (the term "director" is normally used now) have little latitude of action, they may address requests to higher level offices if they find that local needs require accommodation exceeding the quotas assigned to them.

To meet the credit needs of large enterprises that have plants or other establishments in various parts of the country, one local branch of the State Bank is designated as the main servicing office for each such enterprise. It centralizes the enterprise's accounting and the analysis of its financial performance, provides for the inclusion of its projected aggregate credit and currency needs in the national plan, and allocates to the various other local offices involved—those in whose territory the concern's individual establishments are located—limits for credit extensions and cash withdrawals in accordance with applicable overall quotas.

The composition of the State Bank's staff differs from that of either central or commercial banks in the Western countries. Since it is the settlements center and performs important control functions, the State Bank employs a large number of bookkeepers, accountants, and inspectors, in addition to those employees engaged in purely routine operations (such as cash, fiscal agency, and collection operations). But its staff, down to the local level, includes also a large proportion of trained economists, who typically specialize in specific industries. Credit work and the preparation of cash plans require intimate familiarity with the industries serviced by the local office; verification of the broad range of information submitted in support of cash plans and credit applications makes it necessary for staff members to have frequent contacts with their counterparts in individual enterprises, economic organizations, and government units and often to check and negotiate on the spot.

Banking organizations in all countries of Eastern Europe suffer from chronic shortages of properly trained personnel. To a large extent, the staffs of the various banking institutions are trained in special "financial institutes", which in many ways are similar to the finance departments of our schools of business administration. In the Soviet Union, the State Bank directly operates a network of specialized training schools, administered by a special department at the head office; efforts to upgrade the bank's staff, particularly its professional staff, have been greatly intensified in recent years.

OTHER BANKS

Investment Banks, which exist in all the countries except Czechoslovakia, are primarily administrative organizations for the disbursement of budgetary funds on a nonreturnable grant basis in conformity with the approved investment plan and cost estimates; their concern with the funds they disburse ceases as soon as the project financed is completed. Normally their responsibilities entail detailed supervision of construction, of equipment installation, and of the related flow and stocking of building materials and machinery. As an auxiliary activity, they provide short-term credit to the construction industry. This is the sole exception to the State Bank's monopoly of short-term credit, but it is considered logical to assign to Investment Banks the task of extending working-capital loans to the construction industry since a very large proportion of that industry's working capital consists of inventories of building materials which are about to become embodied in the fixed capital of a variety of industries. In general, except with regard to farm cooperatives, the bulk of fixed investment is financed through Investment Bank disbursements.

Investment Banks usually have only a limited number of regional offices. Where necessary, they attach one or several of their own staff to local offices of the State Bank. They keep their funds on deposit with the State Bank and use its cash and accounting services. It is not clear whether the broad shift from grant to loan financing already initiated in several countries is likely to result in a change in the operations of the Investment Banks or in a gradual transfer of their activities to the State Bank.

Other specialized banks exist in areas requiring special attention—agriculture and foreign trade. They are useful for foreign trade because that activity involves continuous business contacts with commercial and central banks outside the communist sphere and hence requires special skills, including familiarity with foreign banking methods. Agriculture is a problem area, although not to the same degree in all the countries. The proportion of agriculture that is socialized varies from country to country, ranging from as little as 10 per cent in Poland to almost 100 per cent in the Soviet Union. State farms are run and financed very much as all other state enterprises. Cooperative farms have a varying, but now generally increasing, degree of independence in setting their production plans, in disposing of their output, and in managing their financial affairs.

Agricultural Banks have usually focused their activities on the financing of investments by cooperative farms. Separate Agricultural Banks now exist only in Poland and East Germany, but their reestablishment in Rumania is under consideration. The Soviet Union and most of the other countries have found it expedient to handle both short-term and long-term credit to agriculture through the State Bank.

Foreign Trade Banks exist in all the countries except Rumania—some having been established, or reestablished, in recent years by giving independent status to the foreign department of the State Bank. They maintain correspondent relationships with foreign banks, administer bilateral payments agreements, and maintain foreign exchange facilities for tourists, diplomats, and other foreigners. Foreign exchange operations are usually shared between the State Bank and the Foreign Trade Bank, but in Czechoslovakia and Poland, two countries with large emigration before World War II, there exist special Foreign Exchange Banks, which handle remittances to local residents at preferential exchange rates. The organization and activities of the Foreign Trade and Foreign Exchange Banks and their relationships with the monobank and the International Bank for Economic Cooperation are more fully discussed in Chapter 7.

Savings banks, which are discussed in Chapter 6, play an important and growing role in Eastern Europe. They are the only banking facility available to the population at large—to individuals and also to the small entrepreneurs and independent craftsmen (except in countries where farmers and craftsmen have access to credit cooperatives). In some countries they have only depository functions, and in others they engage in lending as well.

Over the years the banking structure of each communist country has undergone various organizational changes. These have involved the creation of new institutions and mergers of existing ones, important changes in the internal structure of the existing banks, mainly the State Bank, and reassignment of responsibilities, both between the State Bank and the specialized banks and within the latter group. The most important changes will be discussed briefly in Part II and also in Chapter 8. The broad recent trend has been toward greater centralization. Thus the Czechoslovak Investment Bank was abolished in 1959, its functions going to the State Bank, and in the same year several institutions in the Soviet Union were consolidated into a single Investment Bank. In Hungary and Rumania, banks for agriculture were consolidated (in 1954 and 1960) with their respective State Banks, which now share with the savings banks (Hungary) or the Investment Bank (Rumania) the responsibility for extending agricultural credits.

3. The Monetary System and the Payments Flow

In the communist countries, money is created in the same way as in capitalist countries—through the extension of bank credit. This fact is not generally recognized or accepted in the various countries of Eastern Europe. The result is that a good deal of confusion emerges from their economic literature with regard to the nature of money and the role of the monetary process and the function of the banking system. The monetary literature and the pronouncements of banking officials of the Soviet Union are replete with assertions that the lending capacity of the State Bank is limited by available resources, that currency alone is money, and that it is a characteristic of the socialist credit system that money is put into circulation only to support the movement of goods, thus making inflationary processes impossible. A good deal of confusion still exists in the Soviet Union (considerably less so in the other communist countries, notably Poland) as to the proper definition of the money supply. Since Marx identified money with gold, the official theory holds paper money to be merely a substitute for gold and ignores deposit money.[1] Discussion about money is still mostly discussion about currency and is unrelated to credit. The official Soviet view, for instance, is that "credit [paper] money in actual circulation in socialist countries merely represents gold. The quantity of money in circulation is, as a rule, limited by the demand of the national economy for real money—gold".[2]

MONEY IN THE COMMUNIST COUNTRIES

This study will not discuss in detail how the monetary and credit system of the communist countries is related to Marx's views on money (expressed in the context of the earlier stages of the capitalist economy, of course) or the role that the quantity theory of money and the real bills doctrine have played in the formation of Soviet monetary thinking and in that of the other countries of Eastern Europe since World War II. It suffices to recognize that, despite the confusion on the nature of credit and money, and official statements notwithstanding, the monetary system of the communist countries represents a classic case of fiat money, the internal value of which is maintained by administrative controls over its supply.

Domestic money of no communist country is freely convertible into the money of any capitalist or of any other communist country. In the official publications of the Soviet Union the stress on the link of the ruble to gold is pushed to extremes, but there are no legal provisions to implement this link, except to define the gold content of the unit of the national currency. Writings on the subject show a studied ambiguity, of which a statement in a booklet recently published in the Soviet Union is typical: "The exchange value of the ruble and its gold content are determined by the Soviet state on a planned basis, taking into account a set of complex economic factors".[3] Specific references to gold backing either have not been included in the statutes of the State Banks or have been dropped from

---

[1] *See the interesting discussion by the late Hungarian economist Stefan Varga, "Das Geld im Sozialismus", Weltwirtschaftliches Archiv, No. 2, 1957.*

[2] *I. P. Aizenberg,* Osnovy ustoichivosti deneg pri sotsializme *(The Foundations of the Stability of Money Under Socialism), Moscow, 1964; for recent discussion on the role of gold in communist countries and on foreign exchange problems, see also Z. Atlas, "The Socialist Monetary System", D. K., August 1965. However, for a different view, see M. Pessel's "The Bank and the Profit of an Enterprise", D. K., April 1966.*

[3] *V. Trubenkov,* Valiutno-obmennye operatsii v SSSR *(Foreign Exchange Operations in the USSR), Moscow, 1963, page 13.*

them in recent revisions (in Poland in 1958, the USSR in 1960, and Rumania and East Germany in 1965). Where such references are still part of the statute they are general and vague, typically stating merely that note issue is "backed by gold and other assets". And no information is published currently by any communist country on its gold and foreign exchange reserves.

In most countries of Eastern Europe, all currency is issued by the State Bank. In the Soviet Union, however, coin and the smaller denomination currency (one to five rubles) are issued by the Treasury, and in Rumania and Czechoslovakia the Treasury also issues notes; the reason for this latter arrangement is purely historical, and is devoid of any practical significance, since the notes are carried as a liability of the State Bank, and not of the Treasury.

THE MONEY SUPPLY

In the communist as in the capitalist countries, it is proper to regard all current deposits and note liabilities of the banking system as money. As a practical matter, however, one is confronted with several difficulties. First, the gradual enlargement of resources of the State Bank (and of the entire banking system) occurs mainly in the same way as capital formation in the whole government-owned sector of the economy—essentially through the budget; in the particular case of the State Bank, this takes principally the form of budget surpluses left with it on deposit (while the bank's capital is usually enlarged by retention of a fixed share, typically one half, of its profits). These balances represent cumulative surpluses of past years and are thus tantamount to additions to bank capital, or at least to frozen balances, and not to banking claims. On the other hand, since savings banks are in effect the only institutions that provide banking services for the population, including transfer and payments services, and the only depository of the population's liquid balances, all or a portion of the savings bank deposits should be considered part of the active money supply, and a consolidated statement of the monetary system ought to include such banks. Finally, balances of all or some enterprises of the socialized sector may be temporarily sterilized, or their use may be restricted by administrative decision; thus the aggregate level of such balances at any given point of time has only limited meaning. Indeed, in the communist countries, the quantity of money (as contrasted with currency in circulation) is not a policy objective and total money supply is not considered to have any analytical significance.

The quantity of money is increased not through the mechanism of multiple credit expansion on the basis of the acquisition of international reserves (or domestic gold production) or the monetization of domestic debt, but rather by a planned expansion of currency in circulation and of bank credit to the economy, calculated to match the planned increase in the national product and taking into account any changes in its distribution. Since all cash balances of the economy (except currency held by households and petty cash by enterprises) are held by one single bank, there can be no secondary credit expansion. The amount of deposit balances depends largely on central policy decisions, including planned changes in inventories, though it is affected also by such factors as unplanned changes in the velocity of currency circulation and disruptions in the flow of book-entry payments in the government-owned sector.

Making money a tool of administrative controls as well as a means of payment has resulted in the creation of a complex and cumbersome payments system. Delays resulting from the time consumed in verification and accounting complexities have been compounded by requiring that specified payments techniques be used for certain categories of transactions: although the payer has a choice in certain cases, as a rule the nature of the transaction dictates the way in which the payment must be made. By requiring documentary evidence of performance to accompany each order to pay, and for other reasons, the use of checks as a means of payment has been reduced to a minimum in business transactions. As a result, the banking system of the Soviet Union has been engaged for decades in endless attempts to develop an efficient payments mechanism, though denying itself the simple solution of a national check-clearing system (as in the United States) or some combination of such a system with a centralized transfer (giro) system (as in most countries of Western Europe). Only in recent years have attempts been made in several countries of Eastern Europe to make greater use of checks and to find ways of combining their use with the complex controls that form an integral part of all payments flows. Originally the other Eastern European countries copied the Soviet system of payments, thus supplanting their existing payments arrangements, which to varying degrees made use of checks for business payments, but they seem to have avoided some of the Soviet system's complexities, and in recent years they have made greater strides toward simplification.

As was pointed out in Chapter 1, all domestic transactions in communist countries are separated into two payments circuits, though the two circuits are interrelated. The rationale for the separation is mainly its usefulness in monetary planning and control. The State Bank is the focal point of the two flows, and their management absorbs a large part of the staff's energies, particularly at the local office level.

THE CURRENCY CIRCUIT

In the countries of Eastern Europe, the money income of the nonfarm population is paid in currency (except for a relatively small amount of direct deposits into savings accounts in the Soviet Union and some other countries). Collectivized farmers receive part of their income in kind and the balance in currency. Farmers, including those in collective (cooperative) and state farms, receive currency also through direct sales of produce to other consumers. In the Soviet Union (and perhaps elsewhere), collective farms and other types of farm cooperatives are not required to hold all their free cash with the State Bank, although great efforts are made to induce them to bank their cash receipts. (In the Soviet Union, collective farmers bank only 20 per cent to 70 per cent of their sales receipts, depending on the region.)

Thus the growth of currency in circulation in communist countries is a function not only of growth of real income and of changes in the price level, but also of the changing relative sizes of the socialized and the private sectors. Also, the relationship between the state and the collective farms has been subject to changes over time. In the Soviet Union the remonetization of relations between the farm sector and the state during the post-Stalin era has significantly increased the volume of currency flows. The growing tendency in the Soviet Union and other countries to shift the remuneration of the members of cooperative farms from an annual distribution of income on the basis of work performed, measured in "work-day units", to current payment of rewards fixed in monetary terms increases the volume of money circulation within the rural population and the velocity of its turnover. The initiation of pension payments to farmers (and increases in other pensions) in the Soviet Union at the beginning of 1965 had a similar effect. Various increases in pensions and other social insurance payments, and steps taken in several countries of Eastern Europe to reduce subsidies for rent or public services, have also tended to increase currency flows. In countries where a relatively large part of agricultural production remains in private hands, and where private production of other goods and services is more significant than in the Soviet Union, the importance of production payments made in currency is relatively large.

While currency normally returns to the State Bank office after only one trans-

46

action (when currency paid out as wages is spent in retail stores and redeposited by them with the bank), a certain part of the currency paid out to the population changes hands within the population itself, with one group purchasing goods and services from another. Four main kinds of transactions within the private sector are consummated through the use of currency: payments for services, sales by artisans and cooperative producers, sales of second-hand goods, and direct sales by farmers. Of these, the last is the most important.

Products purchased directly from farmers substitute for part of the goods and services that urban consumers would otherwise have purchased from the socialized sector; on the other hand, farmers use the proceeds of market sales to the urban population to acquire goods and services. Such shifts (and changes in the value of privately produced goods and services) may require adjustments in the bill of goods produced for the consumer sector, as the items demanded by farmers may differ from those preferred by the urban population. But as long as claims on the socialized sector are merely transferred from one group of private claimants to another, few problems arise for the money managers and planners.

Continuous efforts are made to prevent consumers from hoarding currency. Such hoards tend to feed black market and other illicit activities and also make possible sudden surges of spending that could create shortages in retail stores. Such situations have arisen in several countries at various times: for instance when the people of Poland, in the fall of 1956, tried to stock up on food as a reaction to the events in Hungary, or when a currency conversion or an increase in official prices was expected in that country, as in October 1963. One frequently encounters the official accusation that "enemies of the people" have attempted to create political difficulties by using hoarded currency to stock up on goods and thus to create shortages of consumer goods. The official desire to reduce the amount of currency in circulation is revealed by the emphasis placed in recent years on the use of savings accounts, on the automatic depositing of salaries in such accounts, and on the use of the savings bank transfers (in preference to currency) for making rent, utility, and similar payments.

Prompt recapturing of the largest possible amount of currency put into circulation is one of the shibboleths of monetary management in the communist countries. In all of them, inordinate emphasis is placed on channeling the cash receipts of trade and service establishments into State Bank offices as promptly as possible and on minimizing the amount of till cash that such establishments, and also industrial establishments, are permitted to hold. Any inflow of currency that results in vault cash holdings ("operating reserves") exceeding stipulated

47

levels results in transfers to the centrally controlled "general reserve", from which notes and coins can be released only on specific orders from the main and regional offices. Elaborate precautions are taken to avoid issuance of currency except in strict conformity with the cash plan (see Chapter 4), and unissued notes are placed under strict central control.

THE NONCASH CIRCUIT

In the state sector, all payments are through transfers on the books of the State Bank, with insignificant exceptions.[4] Two main types of payments may be distinguished. One, closely geared to the flow of materials and services, involves payments among government-owned enterprises that are engaged in the production of goods and services. The other type consists of payments between the enterprises and the budget, those among the various units of government, and those of organizations not operated for profit. In the Soviet Union, the first category accounts for more than four fifths of all noncash payments.

All enterprises are required to make daily deposits of their currency receipts (incoming currency that is not to be disbursed directly) and to keep their balances with the State Bank (or, when appropriate, a specialized bank). Control is further facilitated by the requirement that each enterprise keep its accounts with only one specified banking office—that in whose territory it is located. Under the standard system each enterprise maintains one basic current (clearing) account, in which all its uncommitted funds are held, and separate loan accounts. Originally, in the Soviet Union, a separate account was established for each loan, and this arrangement was copied elsewhere, along with other aspects of Soviet banking; more recently, there has been a tendency to merge these separate accounts into a general (global) loan account. Trade establishments (and some others as well) must pay all sales proceeds into the loan account, or must transfer a specified part of sales proceeds from the clearing account, in order to repay loans. A further step toward the simplification of payments flows is a move in the Soviet Union to merge the clearing and loan accounts of enterprises in certain industries. (See, however, the different arrangements introduced in Rumania, Chapter 11.)

---

[4] *Payments that do not exceed certain limits—100 rubles in the Soviet Union, 1,500 zlotys in Poland, and so on—may be made in currency. And trade organizations are authorized, in strictly circumscribed situations, to make payments in cash for certain purchases.*

48

The essential principle of the system of payments flows within the state enterprise sector is the automatic recovery of working capital. Payments are rigidly geared to shipments and to the receipt of drafts accompanied by bills of lading. Goods must be normally paid for, in accordance with a fixed time schedule, shortly after documentary drafts are received by purchasers. Payments due are collected at the initiative of the creditor, by his submitting to the bank a payments claim (proof of shipment or document covering goods in transit). As long as the shipment is in conformity with the economic plan, and with contracts based on the plan, and the shipping documents have been submitted to the bank, the buyer must pay the draft whether or not the goods shipped have been actually received.

Presumably to facilitate control over each transaction, monthly or other periodic billings are not used, and hence each single transaction involves a separate payment. As a result, the number of separate payments for a given output of goods and services is much larger than in capitalist countries, putting an unnecessary transfer and accounting burden on the banking system.[5] The inefficiency of the current payments system is now widely recognized in Eastern Europe, and efforts are being made to find a system that would reduce paperwork and costs.

Sales receipts not absorbed by the payment of wages (in currency) and for the purchase of materials (through book transfers to other enterprises) are paid into the budget (also through book transfers, usually involving complex allocation formulas). These payments, representing taxes and a substantial proportion of amortization and profits, are normally made automatically by the State Bank at frequent intervals (in some cases every five days or weekly), and if necessary they are financed through bank loans to the enterprise. When cash balances are inadequate to meet all payments, a strict and complex system of priorities comes into play, with currency withdrawals for wage payments usually having first priority (provided these are within the limits of the planned wages fund or are related to production in excess of the plan), after allowing a small amount for "urgent needs" (in the Soviet Union up to 5 per cent of daily receipts). Next in priority are payments to the government, followed by payments into depreciation reserves, by loan repayments, and finally by all other claims, including those of suppliers. Even in the Soviet Union doubts are now being expressed about the

---

[5] *Recent studies by the Ministry of Finance of East Germany indicate that 40 per cent of business transfer payments in that country involve amounts of less than 200 marks ($90 at the official rate). In the Soviet Union, nearly one third of all payments transfers involve amounts of less than 100 rubles ($111).*

wisdom of this system; in Rumania it was given up as early as 1958.

Any slippage between the flow of receipts and payments tends to be reflected in difficulties in meeting interenterprise obligations. Thus a primary task of the banking system is to provide for a smooth payments (deposit transfer) mechanism that will promptly return to the enterprise all working funds spent in producing the output delivered to the next link in the chain and that will provide credit for bridging payment gaps (see Chapter 5).

PAYMENTS INSTRUMENTS

While all interenterprise payments take the form of transfers on the books of the State Bank (as do payments into the budget), several different instruments are used to effectuate such transfers. The terms designating these instruments are similar to those used in the Western world, but their legal form and the content of the transactions are quite different. In all communist countries the main forms for making interenterprise payments (unless offsets are used) are documentary drafts, letters of credit, and cashier's checks. These three general forms, developed in the Soviet Union, have certain variants in the other countries, but without change in the basic principles involved.

By far the most widely used means of paying for interenterprise purchases is the documentary draft, called "acceptance" in Eastern Europe. These drafts are used, in particular, when continuous relationships are involved; such semi-permanent trade relations are usual in Soviet-type economies, in which there is a single source for each major material and most of the output is sold through outlets determined by planners. A "subsequent acceptance" draft is sent by the seller to the office of the State Bank which has his account. That office makes collection by forwarding the demand for payment to the bank office that handles the buyer's account, which normally enters a corresponding debit the same day the seller's claim is received. Then, within a specified period, the buyer can refuse payment by asking the bank to reverse entries and to reinstate the status quo ante. Refusals to accept payment demands are not numerous in relation to the total; in recent years they have accounted in the Soviet Union (including partial refusals) for only about 2 per cent of all "subsequent acceptance" drafts. A variant of this method involves "prior acceptance" by the drawee, but the automatic method is the more usual, with the buyer having the right to seek subsequent adjustments and refunds. One of the frequently criticized aspects of this procedure—which is clearly designed to achieve prompt payment—is that the buyer's account is sometimes debited even before he has taken delivery and has had an opportunity to examine the shipment.

In the case of infrequent purchases, in particular those from distant suppliers, letters of credit are used to assure prompt payment, with the buyer's account debited at the time the letter is issued. Cashier's checks (generally issued in the form of booklets of checks for a stated total amount) are used mostly to pay for services or when the precise amount due cannot be determined in advance. The requirement that each freight bill be settled separately and immediately illustrates the extreme to which the general principle is pushed that payments for all goods and services must be prompt in order to restore the working capital of the seller. Finally, transfer orders are used to pay profits and taxes into the budget and to transfer funds among the budgets of administrative units at various levels of government, while ordinary checks are used mainly to withdraw payroll cash from the banks.

Recently, a variety of attempts have been made in several countries to abandon the basic principle of semiautomatic payments. These attempts are motivated by a desire to assure that goods shipped conform better with specifications, to improve the quality of production and speed up deliveries, to avoid the occasional need to make payment before delivery, and more generally to give the buyer greater control. There is, of course, considerable room for making payments arrangements more flexible and efficient without infringing on the other significant aspects of the payments system, but there does not seem to be any intention of relieving the State Bank of the tremendous accounting work involved in distributing sales proceeds (and other receipts) among the various statutory accounts (amortization, profits, turnover tax, and the shares of the various levels of government in certain taxes) as well as the separate loan accounts where such accounts are still used.

East Germany has pioneered in abandoning the system of automatic payments for goods shipped. There, as in all the other countries to various degrees, depending on the success achieved in increasing the output of consumer goods, the need to afford protection to the buyer has been increased by changes that have occurred in recent years. As was succinctly stated in a recent article in the official publication of the State Bank of the Soviet Union:[6]

---

[6] G. Moiseenko, "Concerning the New System of Payments in the German Democratic Republic", D. K., July 1965, pages 72-73.

In the past, when many goods were in short supply, the relationship between industry and trade was relatively simple. Trade required the delivery of large quantities of goods. Industrial establishments could dispose of their output without difficulty. Now the situation is quite different. The buyer does not take everything without choosing. He chooses goods that are fashionable, cheap, and of good quality.

In East Germany, prior to 1965, payment through acceptances accounted, as in the other countries, for the overwhelming bulk, about 85 per cent, of inter-enterprise payments. The new system, which was introduced on January 1, 1965, after being tested in limited areas over a period of time, gives individual enterprises the right to stipulate in a sales contract the method of payment that will apply, including payment by check or by transfer; the State Bank, which formerly determined the method of payment, now does so only in exceptional cases. Payment by check or transfer permits the buyer to exercise greater control over the quality of goods delivered as well as over delivery terms. He no longer sees his account debited on a fixed schedule, even when he has had no opportunity to examine and accept the shipment—although automatic debiting is maintained when verification of the goods delivered or the services provided is either unnecessary or impracticable (as, for instance, in utilities or for services provided by municipalities, etc.). Letters of credit continue to be used only where no continuing relationship exists, or for buyers whose bad payments record warrants special treatment. Standard terms have been established for payment by check or transfer, but they can be modified by the contracting parties. A stiff penalty rate (equivalent to 18 per cent per year) is established for overdue payments. The amount of work involved in making small payments has been reduced by shifting payments of less than 200 marks to the postal checking system, with which each enterprise is required to open an account for this purpose. It has been found that payments made in this way cost only slightly more than half the expense of a book-entry transfer at the State Bank.

The possibility of making a similar shift from transfers to checks is now under active study in the Soviet Union. Tests conducted in several Soviet cities have shown that the use of checks not only is cheaper and more convenient but actually results in greater promptness of payments.

4. Monetary and Credit Plans

Although the basic planning in the communist countries is in real terms, output goals must be translated into monetary terms. The cash, credit, and investment financing needed to implement a given output plan must be spelled out and meshed. Thus the national monetary plans—on which the activities of the State Bank and of all other banks are based—are the counterparts of economic plans articulated in physical magnitudes.[1]

All plans discussed in this chapter are tied together in an overall financial plan, usually prepared at the Ministry of Finance or by the central planning authority, which shows intersector financial flows, particularly the sources of investment funds and in some cases the use of credit in the economy. As a rule the overall plan takes the form of a sources-and-uses-of-funds statement, prepared on an annual basis and for the country as a whole. Its purpose is to make certain that projected uses and available resources will balance; its main component parts are the national budget and the credit and cash plans of the State Bank. As a sample, the articulation of the Financial Plan of Czechoslovakia is shown in Table 1.

The government budget, in addition to determining the volume and distribution of centrally channeled investment funds, indicates the amount of resources allocated to the banking system for extending medium- and long-term loans and the amount of surpluses expected to accumulate at the State Bank. The plans of the monetary and banking system itself—the credit and cash plans—are prepared by the State Bank and are designed to accommodate the economy's needs for currency and credit while preserving price stability. Two of the principal activities of the State Bank—extension of credit and management of currency circulation—are based on these plans, which are tantamount to internal operating documents. They guide the day-to-day activities of the banking system and provide the formal framework for current reporting on its activities. This comprehensive and current reporting, in turn, permits the monitoring of the actual performance of the economy in relation to the projected path. Although they are interrelated, the banking plans are sufficiently different in form, time

---

[1] *For additional discussion of the history of monetary plans in the Soviet Union, see the author's "The Role of the State Bank in Soviet Planning",* Soviet Planning: Essays in Honor of Naum Jasny, *edited by Jane Degras and Alec Nove (Oxford: Basil Blackwell, 1964).*

horizon, method of preparation, and territorial detail to warrant separate discussion.

TABLE 1

THE FINANCIAL PLAN (CZECHOSLOVAKIA)

Resources	*Uses*
Government-owned enterprises:	Government-owned enterprises:
Profits	Investments and capital maintenance
Depreciation allowances	Housing construction (part included in the national plan)
Other revenues	Other expenditures
Decrease in working capital	Increase in working capital
Profits and depreciation allowances of financial and insurance institutions	Noninvestment government expenditures (such as health and social welfare, defense, and administration)
Turnover tax	
Other taxes and fees	
Social insurance receipts	
Other government revenues	
Resources of special budgetary organizations	Noninvestment needs of special budgetary organizations
Decrease in domestic inventories	Increase in domestic inventories
Decrease in credits to agricultural and other cooperatives	Increase in credits to agricultural and other cooperatives
Consumer savings	Expenditures of the population exceeding the plan
Increase in banking and commercial indebtedness to foreign countries	Decrease in banking and commercial indebtedness to foreign countries
	Increase in credits granted abroad
Balance-of-payments deficit	Balance-of-payments surplus
	Reserves
Other resources	Other needs
Total resources	**Total uses**
Deficiency of resources	Excess of resources

Source: Basic Questions of the Financial Economy of the Czechoslovak Socialist Republic, *Prague, 1965. In the interest of greater clarity, the items have been rearranged and in some cases their designation has been translated into Western terms.*

54

THE SHORT-TERM CREDIT PLAN

The Credit Plan,[2] an important component of the overall economic plan of each communist country, determines the increase in short- and medium-term credit to be made available to the economy during the period of the plan. It is prepared by the State Bank and is essentially a sources-and-uses-of-funds statement cast in terms of outstanding balances projected for the end of the period. Basically, the Credit Plan is derived by combining the projected credit needs of all enterprises with the amounts allocated for extending credit to collective farms, to individuals, and where applicable to independent farmers and private entrepreneurs. Short-term credits to the construction industry, extended by the Investment Bank, and credits for exports, extended by the Foreign Trade Bank, are usually included in it, though for operational purposes separate plans for these specialized banks are also prepared. Marginal changes during the period of the plan are projected for each sector of the economy (industry, trade, agriculture) and by purpose (such as seasonal needs, inventories, advances on collection float). As an example, the structure of the Credit Plan used in the Soviet Union is shown in Table 2. It follows strictly administrative lines (reflecting the successive addition of new "objects of crediting"), with no attempt at a functional or analytical presentation.

Outsiders' knowledge of the plan itself is limited to its structure (stubs and column headings), since neither its projections nor its actuals are published. Only scant information is available on the relative contributions of the various sources of funds—the budget, changes in bank capital and reserves, deposit balances of enterprises, net changes in currency in circulation, and so on. On the uses of funds, however, most countries publish actual figures, at least on an annual basis, usually by purpose and main industry categories and in some cases by territorial subdivisions. Thus it is possible to analyze at least the broad changes in the volume and structure of credit in use. Indeed, these data represent the most significant body of monetary information regularly published by the countries of Eastern Europe.

Before the recent trend toward decentralization, which allows the branches of the State Bank greater participation in credit planning, the process of planning

---

[2] *In contrast to the plan for long-term credit, described in the following section, that for short-term credit is usually referred to briefly as "the Credit Plan".*

TABLE 2

THE SHORT-TERM CREDIT PLAN OF THE STATE BANK (USSR)

Sources of funds	*Uses of funds*
Capital, reserves, and profits	Loans secured by inventories and for seasonal needs
Government balances (all levels)	Loans for new technology
Balances of economic units and collection float	Loans for increasing output of consumer goods
Balances of nonprofit organizations	Loans against drafts in the process of collection
Balances of credit institutions*	Loans to bridge payments gaps
Currency in circulation	Loans for temporary needs
Other	Loans for the payment of wages
	Reserve for allocation by head office
	Other†
Total	**Total**

---

* *Savings and specialized banks.*

† *Bank buildings and other property, currency in vaults and in transit, foreign exchange, precious metals.*

Source: M. B. Bogachevskii, Finansy i kredit v SSSR *(Finances and Credit in the USSR), Moscow, 1964, page 271.*

changes in credit volume involved little more than centralizing the credit requests of the various enterprises and setting proper criteria for checking their conformity with established (but not necessarily immutable) crediting norms. Credit demands were presented to the State Bank on a consolidated basis—usually quarterly, except for agriculture—by the ministries or administrations in charge of each branch of industry. The Credit Plan was an almost automatic by-product of the collation of these claims by industry and purpose, with a certain amount of scaling-down of the original requests. In the Soviet Union, about half of all short-term credit is still centrally planned at the head office on the basis of these claims presented by ministries or economic administrations, but the percentage is apparently considerably lower in Poland and Czechoslovakia, where the State Bank's credit planning has been decentralized. In general, the planning of inventory (including seasonal) loans is now left to the monobank's branches, while the amounts earmarked for settlement credits and for various needs that cannot be foreseen in advance continue to be planned centrally, with specific quotas ("limits") for the various major purposes distributed to individual regional and local offices.

To the extent that resources for lending are derived from budget surpluses and from the increase in currency circulation, their use can be planned only nationally. Such resources allocated from the main office are supplemented in each territorial and local branch by balances maintained by the enterprises and lower level governmental units whose accounts these offices carry.

The Credit Plan is broken down into territorial plans, extending to the lowest administrative unit, which combine credit allocations planned centrally with those made by the local or regional offices. The articulation of Credit Plans by purpose, which originally comprised only two categories (financing of inventories and collection items), has grown with the introduction of new "objects of crediting" (see Chapter 5). Further changes in the format of the plans have occurred from time to time as a result of major changes in the organization of the administration of the economy. And, since the introduction in the mid-1950's of medium-term loans to finance improvements in technology, the Credit Plan has been restructured in most countries to show separately the amounts provided for medium-term lending.

The method of preparing the Credit Plan differs, although not significantly, from country to country. In Bulgaria, Poland, and Rumania, as in the Soviet Union, plans are prepared quarterly (in Rumania, they are further broken down by months); in Czechoslovakia, East Germany, and Hungary, plans are constructed annually and subsequently broken down by quarters. In addition, longer term Credit Plans are prepared in Czechoslovakia (five years), Rumania (six years), and East Germany (seven years). The need for quarterly Credit Plans arises in part from the seasonal character of production and in part to provide a basis for checking the performance of individual enterprises. Also, unforeseen divergences from planned output schedules and inventory goals may require corrective measures, including alteration of plans. For example, an overfulfillment of planned targets in a given consumer goods industry may result in increased deliveries of such goods to wholesale organizations, which then need more credit to carry them than had been anticipated.

The Credit Plan must be approved by a higher authority, which in most countries, including the USSR, is the Council of Ministers. It then becomes a binding government "directive" in the areas of short-term credit and currency circulation. The whole evaluation of the role played by such a plan hinges on the significance of this directive for the actual operations of the banking system. Available evidence suggests that the Credit Plan is in reality little more than a set of projections consistent with the material plans and capable of providing guidelines for the credit activities of the banking system. The "planned" totals are, in effect, permissible limits rather than targets to be achieved. The fact that they are more frequently achieved and exceeded than "underfulfilled" reflects general inflationary tendencies and the desire to keep large inventories as a protection against unforeseen but recurrent disruptions and slowdowns in the circular flow of goods.

THE LONG-TERM CREDIT PLAN

In addition to the plan for short-term (including medium-term) credit, the State Bank prepares a separate plan for its long-term lending. Since such plans involve the financing of fixed investment, with most projects requiring several years for

TABLE 3

THE LONG-TERM CREDIT PLAN (USSR)

Sources of funds	Uses of funds
Loan repayments:	Loans granted:
Collective farms*	Collective farms*
Farm population	Farm population
Individuals†	Individuals†
Consumer cooperatives	Consumer cooperatives
Municipal enterprises	Municipal enterprises
Budgetary resources:	Repayment of temporary Treasury loans
For enlarging the long-term credit fund	
Temporary loans from the Treasury‡	
Subsidies of Union republics§	

---

* Including construction enterprises servicing collective farms.

† Loans for home construction in nonurban areas.

‡ To meet seasonal peaks.

§ Provided for meeting part of the cost of houses built to accommodate internal migrants.

Sources: M. M. Usoskin, Organizatsiia i planirovanie kredita (Organization and Planning of Credit), Moscow, 1961, page 408; and M. B. Bogachevskii, Finansy i kredit v SSSR (Finances and Credit in the USSR), Moscow, 1964, page 337.

58

completion, they are prepared on an annual basis only. Like the plans for short-term credit, they are, in effect, sources-and-uses-of-funds projections, but instead of showing outstanding balances they indicate gross flows—the amounts to be made available during the year under the various headings; thus no integration of the two plans is possible. The structure of the Soviet long-term credit plan is shown in Table 3.

Long-term credit plans include only repayable loans (not only for productive but also for nonproductive investment, such as housing and municipal services), although in some cases, subsidies to meet part of the cost of the project to be financed are also channeled through the plan. In addition to repayments, the sources of funds shown in the plan normally include budgetary resources—articulated by earmarked purpose, such as financing of agriculture, home building, and so on. Where separate Investment Banks exist, or where other specialized banks extend a certain amount of long-term credit, their activities of this kind may (as in the Soviet Union) or may not be consolidated in the overall plan prepared by the State Bank. Again, the plans are not published, but historical data on long-term lending are available for most countries. Until the partial shift from grant to loan financing in industry was initiated in the early sixties, financing of investment in agriculture, particularly by farm cooperatives, represented the bulk of long-term credit granted in the communist countries. (For an example of a single credit plan, combining working capital and investment credit, see Chapter 13.)

BALANCE OF MONEY INCOMES AND EXPENDITURES OF THE POPULATION

Planning of currency circulation involves determination of the additional amounts to be put into (or retired from) circulation each year without disturbing monetary equilibrium, and also detailed projections of seasonal and geographic variations of currency needs. Quarterly plans for gross currency receipts and payments were developed in the Soviet Union as early as 1930, but until the 1947 currency reform they do not seem to have been successfully enforced. Actually, these were years of price increases of inflationary proportions, and increases in currency in circulation exceeded the planned percentages by large margins during the 1930's. It was only toward the end of that decade, with the more rigid enforcement of wage and other controls, that Gosbank planning and control of currency flows became a significant tool of economic policy.

The "Balance of Money Incomes and Expenditures of the Population" (subsequently referred to as the Balance) is the starting point in preparing the Cash Plan, and it also serves the broader purpose of aiding in planning the

TABLE 4

BALANCE OF MONEY INCOMES AND EXPENDITURES OF THE POPULATION (USSR)

Money incomes	*Money expenditures*
A. Receipts from government and co-operative enterprises and nonprofit organizations: 　Wages and salaries 　Money income of collective farms 　Individuals' receipts from sales of agricultural products* 　Pensions and similar payments 　Stipends (to students, etc.) 　Receipts from the financial system† 　Other income 　Personal money transfers‡	A. Payments to government and cooperative enterprises, nonprofit organizations, and savings: 　Purchases of goods 　Payments for services and other expenditures 　Compulsory and voluntary payments (taxes, contributions, insurance premiums, membership dues) 　Savings (net increase in savings bank balances, purchases of 3 per cent government savings bonds) 　Personal money transfers‡
Subtotal for A	*Subtotal for A*
B. Receipts from sales of goods and services to the population: 　Sales of farm products through collective farm outlets 　Sales of household and other goods and services	B. Payments for purchases of goods and services from the population: 　Purchases of farm products from collective farm outlets 　Purchases of household and other goods and services and other expenditures
Subtotal for B	*Subtotal for B*
Total incomes (A + B)	**Total expenditures (A + B)**
Excess of expenditures over receipts	Excess of receipts over expenditures

* *Sales made to the socialized sector from the private output of collective farm members and individual farmers.*

† *Interest on savings deposits, lottery prizes, insurance payments, loans for housing construction.*

‡ *Largely money orders and letters of credit; included only in balances for individual territories, such as republics and regions.*

Source: M. B. Bogachevskii, Finansy i kredit v SSSR *(Finances and Credit in the USSR), Moscow, 1964, page 285.*

60

production and distribution of consumer goods and services. It consists of a two-part sources-and-uses-of-funds statement: payments flows between the population and the combined socialized sector (Sector A, consisting of economic and administrative units) are distinguished from transactions within the population (Sector B). Its preparation starts as a trial comparison of anticipated disposable income with the projected supply of consumer goods and services, and it ends up as a formal quarterly plan approved by the Council of Ministers or some other high-level authority. It is not a complete statement of the consumer account, since payments in kind (and the imputed value of free services) are not included. Sector A serves as the basis for preparation of the Cash Plan, because transactions in Sector B merely increase the velocity of the currency that is put into circulation through transactions between the socialized sector and the population; only a very small part of Sector B transactions enters into the Cash Plan. The Balance is usually prepared by the national Planning Office. Various sources are used in its preparation, ranging from actuals of the Cash Plan in the preceding period to sample surveys of consumer expenditures. The form of the Balance used in the Soviet Union is shown in Table 4.

There is no doubt that the Balance meets important analytical needs, in part because in the process of its construction the size and origin of prospective disequilibria are revealed. Indeed, the permissible "noninflationary" increase in circulation is determined within an implicit analytical framework that is not unfamiliar to Western economists. Measures to make the two sides of the account balance may involve changes in production, distribution, wages, or prices. Such measures may aim, depending on conditions, at increasing the volume of available resources or reducing their prospective uses, or both, and are taken largely by authorities outside the State Bank; the accounts and the monetary plans of the State Bank merely register the monetary effects of actions initiated elsewhere.

THE CASH PLAN

The Cash Plan, which is the basic operating plan of the State Bank (and hence is broken down to the successive administrative levels), is essentially an abbreviated sources-and-uses-of-funds statement of the consumer sector, derived from the Balance, primarily from its A section. For all practical purposes, the Balance may be regarded as the analytical framework, and the Cash Plan as the operating document, for the State Bank's major efforts to preserve monetary balance. The plan, which is prepared quarterly, serves as the basis for all bank activities involving the issue of currency and also for the elaborate controls over the disbursements of currency. This explains the great emphasis placed on strict adherence to the Cash Plan figures on all administrative levels. The form of the Cash Plan as used in the Soviet Union is given in Table 5.

On the assumption of stable velocity for each of the main categories of consumers, the rise in consumer disposable income that would result from a planned growth in national product yields an estimate of the required "noninflationary" increase in currency in circulation. This estimate determines, in turn, what adjustments are required in the Credit Plan into which it enters as a source of funds. The proper annual change in the amount of currency in circulation is one of the "proportionalities" that are supposed to underlie planning in communist countries and to assure the consistency of the various monetary plans among themselves and with physical plans.

Official sources estimate that in the Soviet Union about 90 per cent of the money income of the population finds its counterpart in currency withdrawn from banks, and that conversely the same percentage of consumer expenditures eventuates in currency receipts by bank offices, since trade and service establishments (with very small exceptions) immediately bank all their receipts. The figure is probably much the same in the other countries. Wages account for about four fifths of the outgo side of the Cash Plan, and thus the latter ties in closely with the wages fund plan, another key element in all communist planning. In the Soviet Union, the Planning Office has been responsible since 1959 for establishing ceilings on wage and salary payments in each republic, and the Gosbank must fit payments within these limits into its cash plans all down the line to the lowest office.

Indeed, the formulation of the Cash Plan requires cooperation of the State Bank with planning organizations and several ministries. Unlike the Credit Plan, however, the preparation of the Cash Plan begins at the local-office level, even though much of the basic information is supplied from the central office. Individual enterprises and government units usually submit their own cash plans—supported by a wide range of factual and analytical data, including actuals for past periods—to the State Bank office with which they hold their accounts. In preparing the cash plan for a territorial division, the data obtained by the local offices are combined with information supplied by the regional bank office. The data obtained locally pertain mostly to projected changes, from current actuals, while the central authorities pass down information on increased

TABLE 5

THE CASH PLAN OF THE STATE BANK (USSR)

Deposits	*Withdrawals*
Retail sales receipts	For wage and other labor income payments
Receipts from railroad, water, and air transportation	For payments for agricultural products and raw materials
Taxes and contributions	From accounts of collective farms
Rents and municipal services	For individual housing construction, consumer and pawnshop loans
Receipts from local transportation	By post offices
Receipts for the accounts of collective farms	By savings banks
Post office receipts	For pension allowances, stipends, and insurance payments
Savings bank receipts	Advances for official travel and for cash disbursements of economic units
Receipts of amusement enterprises	
Receipts from personal service establishments	
Receipts from housing cooperatives	
Other receipts	
Total	**Total**
Excess of withdrawals over deposits (currency put into circulation)	Excess of deposits over withdrawals (withdrawal of currency from circulation)

Source: M. B. Bogachevskii, Finansy i kredit v SSSR *(Finances and Credit in the USSR), Moscow, 1964, page 290.*

needs to be expected from the erection of new factories and from the introduction of new programs, such as changes in farm procurement procedures and prices, or new social benefits. Projects submitted by local offices are reviewed by the supervising offices, and a process of successive reviews, adjustments, and consolidations results in the national plan; its formal structure has undergone only minor changes over the years. The Cash Plan includes the transactions (on a net basis) of the specialized and savings banks and the postal system.

The national Cash Plan is ultimately broken down into detailed plans for each banking office. These plans make provision for issuance of additional currency in specific periods or, as the case may be, for retirement of excessive amounts (and their retention in local vaults or transfer to regional offices). Since the discontinuance in some countries of central government review and approval of quarterly (as contrasted with annual) economic plans, the quarterly Cash Plan (with monthly or even ten-day-period distributions of totals) has become a main instrument for controlling the day-to-day performance of the economy, especially with regard to the consumer sector.

The preparation of the Cash Plan, in particular its territorial breakdown, has encountered many difficulties, notably in the Soviet Union. They are rooted not only in insufficiency of basic information, but also in the fact that in some areas the amount of expenditures may considerably exceed income payments (or vice versa)—as a result of regional differences in spending habits and in the use of consumer credit, tendencies to shop in distant places for goods not available locally, growing travel, changes in turnover velocity, and so on. The difficulties of preparing cash plans for relatively small areas are compounded when farmers and farm cooperatives are given comparative freedom in disposing of their output and can thus sell it in markets or shops outside the given territory. Considerable study is being given, particularly in the Soviet Union, to the problem of interregional currency flows.

THE CURRENCY ISSUE DIRECTIVE

Any net increase in the volume of credit outstanding, if not offset by enlarged deposits, including government deposits, or by additions to the State Bank's capital funds, will result in an increase of currency in circulation. Thus the change in the amount of currency in circulation shown as a balancing item in the Credit Plan will be equal to the same item in the Cash Plan. The planned increase (or, theoretically, decrease) is the object of a "Currency Issue Directive", issued usually by the Council of Ministers. The State Bank implements the directive by allocating the total among the various territories and by enforcing detailed procedures established for the issuance of additional amounts of currency by its offices. In some countries (for instance, in Rumania) there is rigid control by the head office, with the branches required to obtain specific authorization for each issue of additional amounts of currency (and all currency which would raise vault cash above a stipulated level being automatically retired); elsewhere the various branches receive issue quotas, which may be exceeded under certain stipulated conditions but usually only after specific authorization from the center.

Global planning requires detailed reporting. Reams of tables on the fulfillment of the various financial plans are prepared at the State Bank and other banking institutions for the various authorities, such as the Ministry of Finance, the Planning Office, and the Central Committee of the Communist Party, with data on the volume of loans extended, the proportion of loans overdue, cash paid out and redeposited, and so on, and breakdowns by industry and region. But almost all reporting is strictly internal, and the amount of published statistical information is very limited. As is typical for all kinds of statistics published by communist countries, the data cannot easily be fitted together, correlated, or made consistent over time. Frequently, no absolute base is given, but only percentage distributions or percentage changes from year to year, and even these are usually contained in occasional articles or reports rather than in regular publications. None of the *ex ante* financial plans (except the budget) are published, and therefore no comparison is possible between plan and actual performance (to the extent that it is reported).

There is little consistency among the countries as to the kind of monetary and banking data that they do publish. The largest range of data relevant for the analysis of monetary and credit developments is published in Poland; at the other extreme is Rumania, which in spite of its fine statistical tradition hardly releases any banking data whatever. No data are available on currency in circulation (except for Poland and East Germany) or on monetary reserves.

The occurrence of inflationary upsurges at various times in several countries of Eastern Europe—despite the fact that the objective of all financial plans, and particularly of the Cash Plan, is to avoid excessive monetary demand by consumers—suggests that there are enough leakages in the control system and enough weaknesses and uncertainties in the underlying planning to permit pressures to arise within the economy. Primarily through wage payments in excess of planned amounts and through activation of currency hoards it becomes possible for actual spending to exceed the amounts planned *ex ante,* and the result is a significant disequilibrium between monetary demand and the available supply at fixed prices.

The quality of credit planning has also suffered from the fact that enterprises' requests for planned credits have tended to be excessive, while bank officials have tended to reduce to a minimum the amounts they approve—this conflict arising because the bank is in a better negotiating position when dealing with requests for amounts not "in the plan" than it is in extending planned credits, which are automatically available to the client. In addition, the excessive compartmentalization of loans has frequently led to a mere shuffling around of credits—fitting them into open slots and under free margins by falsifying their true purpose and straining regulations. The large volume of overdue loans has added to the difficulty of ascertaining whether the actual pattern of lending corresponds to original intentions, or whether reported figures (and the underlying granting of accommodations) have been "bent" to fit the straitjacket of applicable plans; this "bending" has continued to occur in spite of the attempts in the fifties to make the application of credit plans more flexible by specifically providing for "unplanned credits", for unallocated credit quotas ("reserves" at the disposal of various levels of monobank offices), and for transfers of unused quotas between "objects of crediting", industries, and offices (see Chapter 5).

Similarly, deviations in the execution of the Cash Plan seem to have resulted, in specific instances, from a failure of production to meet planned targets and from various "abnormalities", such as farm supplies that bypass normal channels, wage drift, excessive inventory accumulation, and lags in completing new production facilities. Moreover, the Cash Plan itself tends to suffer from the same shortcomings as the Credit Plan (submission of excessive estimates in the hope of receiving amounts actually desired) and from technical deficiencies in estimating income flows, particularly on a territorial basis. Economic publications, especially those of the State Banks, are full of examples of technical shortcomings and lack of realism in the preparation of the various financial plans.[3]

The importance of financial planning in the communist countries may well be increased, rather than diminished, as a result of the changes now in process—the decentralization of investment decisions and the multiplication of avenues for financing, the shift to loan financing and the increased role of interest, the greater response to consumer preferences, and the increased interest in sectoral sources-and-uses-of-funds and flows-of-funds accounts and similar analytical tools. Financial planning and analysis could easily develop, along the lines of current trends in social accounting in Western countries, toward an integration of income and financial flows. Considerable progress has been made, particularly in Poland, toward developing a double-entry table combining financial flows and gross national product. This analytical table shows credit flows through the

---

[3] *For instance, the monthly review of the Gosbank has mentioned this subject in practically every issue over the last few years.*

economy and intrasectoral financial flows; it also distinguishes the socialized from the private sector and contains a number of other analytically significant breakdowns.[4]

5. Credit Policy

After World War II, in the initial stages of the take-over of most Eastern European countries by communist governments, the existing forms and instruments of bank credit were continued for a time, but their use was adapted to a gradual establishment of government control over the entire economy, including the sectors that were not socialized immediately. In this process there was some room for improvisation, the purpose being to resume and expand industrial production and to prevent disruptions because of shortages of working capital. But banking arrangements of the Soviet type were introduced fairly rapidly, and in the early 1950's the credit techniques of all the communist countries conformed with the system used in the Soviet Union since the credit reforms of 1930-32. By the early fifties the ban on interunit ("commercial") credit had become generally effective and bank lending in conformity with the "five principles of socialist credit" (discussed in the subsequent section), along with centralized credit planning, had become the universal rule in Eastern Europe.

After the events of 1956, which represented the first open challenge to communist rule, some of the countries began to venture into new territory in their economic policies. By the end of 1965, they had introduced various modifications combining macroplanning with elements of a market mechanism, and had come to regard credit as an important "economic lever" and as an alternative to the direction of economic activity through administrative decisions. In the area

---

[4] *See Jeremi Wierzbicki, "The Application of the Input-Output Method in the Tables of Material and Financial Flows", in* Studia Finansowe, *No. 1, Institute of Finance, Warsaw, 1965 (in Polish, with English summary), which contains such a table for 1962. Pioneering work in this field has been done by Professor P. Sulmicki, head of the Research Department of the National Bank of Poland; see his "Bilanse syntetyczne", in* Finanse, *August 1964. See also Professor Z. Fedorowicz, "Problèmes de la planification financière dans une économie socialiste", Académie Polonaise des Sciences, Centre Scientifique à Paris, Conférences, fascicule 45, 1963.*

relevant for this study the recent developments involve a significant departure from the standard system. Yet many features of that system, such as the separation of the two money circuits, are being continued as an organic part of the communist economies. The system is based on concepts, elevated in official Soviet literature to the status of principles, that continue to receive lip service in spite of many gaps between theory and experience in each of the countries involved. This chapter discusses the role and uses of credit in communist economies before they began to be affected by the recent changes in economic policies.

THE FIVE PRINCIPLES OF SOCIALIST CREDIT

According to official doctrine, the basic—and also distinguishing—characteristics of "socialist credit" are that it is planned, specific, secured, repayable, and with a fixed maturity. The textbooks of communist countries, in extolling the virtues of these principles, never inform their readers that, except for the first, they happen to be identical with the "real bills" (self-liquidating loan) doctrine generally discarded in the West. And when the force of circumstances makes it necessary to tolerate a continuous breaching of the principles (as in the widespread instances of overdue loans) or to simply throw them overboard (as with the introduction of credit for payroll purposes), little effort is made to reconcile the new policies with the "immutable" principles.

The stress on the first attribute of credit—its planned nature—is hardly surprising. Little needs to be added to the earlier discussion to emphasize the fact that all credit extension is supposed to occur within the framework of financial plans drawn up to implement plans specified in physical units. In actual practice, as will be seen, such planning not only requires provision for "unplanned credits" but, in effect, frequently results in credit extension in excess of the planned volume.

The nature of socialist credit requires that each loan be made for a specific purpose consistent with the underlying plan, and is identifiable as to end use. Thus, under the initial variant of the standard system, an enterprise obtained a number of separate loans for different specific purposes—such as to finance inventories of each of the major raw materials used, to constitute a fuel reserve, or to bridge the payments gap between the shipment of finished goods and the receipt of payment for that particular shipment. Actually, it is frequently possible for a borrower with an overdue loan in one category (say, inventory of raw

68

materials) to obtain a loan for another purpose (say, for fuel) and to pay off the overdue loan from the proceeds. In Poland there was a particularly flagrant tendency for enterprises to finance "unapproved" inventories from their own working capital and to borrow from the bank to finance activities consistent with the economic plan and eligible for regular bank financing.

The requirements that each loan must be secured by material values (normally, the object of the particular loan) and carry a fixed maturity are, of course, constituent elements of the underlying theory that secured, self-liquidating credit cannot have inflationary effects. Considerable emphasis is placed on the need to have all credit properly collateralized, and in the Soviet Union the adequacy of the collateral is frequently checked by State Bank inspectors in the course of periodic visits to plants and warehouses. The fixed maturity requirement is no more a guarantee of prompt repayment in the communist countries than it is in the capitalist countries, as evidenced by the large volume of overdue loans and of indirect loan renewals when the proceeds of a new loan serve to retire the balance of the original accommodation.

Finally, the principle that the loan must be repayable serves to stress the distinction between credit transactions and grants; the bank official is expected to determine whether an adequate flow of payments will be generated to redeem the loan.

Although the credit rules of the standard system do not permit nonbank lending, a major exception to this ban occurs in the financing of agricultural production. Advances against purchase contracts are obtained by cooperative farms (and, in most countries, by individual farmers) from state organizations in charge of procurement of agricultural output, which in effect act as credit intermediaries. (In the Soviet Union such advances have exceeded in recent years the total amount of short-term credit extended directly to agriculture.) Another exception is the extension of credit by foreign trade organizations to enterprises producing goods for export.

Taken together, the five principles of socialist credit and their actual administration—until the recent wave of reforms—result in arrangements whereby credit is available almost automatically and at a set rate, once a number of conditions stipulated in the applicable plans are fulfilled. The enterprise obtains a loan by filing a request, and the bank official concerned ascertains whether the required conditions are met, that is, whether the credit requested is within the limits set in the plan or whether the nature of the underlying transaction automatically entails the right to obtain credit accommodations. Thus the five principles provide the rationale for detailed administrative controls but no basis for a credit policy aimed at controlling aggregate demand. Moreover, these principles encourage self-deception. Strict adherence to them tends to result in considerable shuffling of accounts to achieve formal compliance with the rules, frequently without regard to the stated economic objectives. In reality, even the ban against interunit credit is not completely effective, as it does not prevent an enterprise from using a supplier's funds by delaying payment.

THE USES OF CREDIT

The basic function of credit in the communist countries is to supplement the working capital with which state-owned enterprises are endowed, that is, the funds needed for current expenditures as contrasted with fixed investment. Except in agriculture the role of credit in capital formation is very minor under the standard system.

Since the overriding goal is fulfillment of physical targets, credit is provided whenever it can help to meet them ("fulfill the plan"). Thus access to official banking institutions does not depend on profits or creditworthiness (in any case, a moot problem where state-owned enterprises are concerned). Indeed, economic plans may provide for some government-owned enterprises to operate at a loss, either temporarily or permanently. Such a state of affairs may reflect an intention not to recover all production costs during the run-in period of a new facility, or a need to subsidize socially desirable production or other activities. Because in Soviet-type economies prices do not reflect relative scarcities, but are set by the authorities on the basis of considerations that are complex and not necessarily consistent (in particular when several different agencies set prices of materials entering into the cost of a given final product), situations may arise wherein an enterprise operates quite efficiently in terms of physical and technical indicators and yet shows a deficit.

As a rule, the working capital of units that operate with a "planned loss" is periodically replenished by the higher echelon authorities, which derive resources for such subsidies from profits of other units or from the national budget; when further funds are needed, for seasonal or other temporary purposes, these units normally obtain credit on the same basis as profit-making enterprises. In contrast, enterprises that fall considerably below performance targets, or fail to meet their financial obligations on schedule, are penalized in various ways (discussed below, in the section on credit sanctions). Actually, however, these weak enterprises may have to be nursed in one way or another, since cutting off access to credit (given the low level of "own" working capital) would in most cases mean inability to continue operations.

The main use of credit is to help enterprises meet seasonal or other temporary needs, primarily to finance inventories and to bridge the transfer gap in the sale of intermediate and final products within and by the socialized sector. Short-term credit for such purposes is of vital importance in the communist economies; it is discussed in some detail in the next section. The other use of short-term credit in the socialized sector is to supplement an enterprise's "own" funds in the interest of growth; this is given brief consideration in the following paragraphs.

When an increase in working capital is needed for growth purposes, that part of the increase not available from the enterprise's retained profits (the excess of sales receipts over direct production costs and taxes) may be provided through allocations from the national budget (or reallocations from the profits of other enterprises) or through credit—or both, in particular when the objective is to maintain a fixed proportion between "own" and borrowed funds.[1] Different policies have been pursued in the various countries, taking into account a variety of considerations but especially the need to maintain tight administrative controls over the financial behavior of all parts of the economy. Credit extended for additional working-capital purposes may be repaid out of future profits or from budgetary grants received in the following year.

But whatever the route by which additional working capital is supplied, its source—except for an increase in note issue—is the socialized part of the national product channeled through the budget. For the maintenance of monetary equilibrium it is of only secondary importance whether such funds are provided directly from profits (or by reallocations among enterprises) or are centralized first in the budget and then distributed as grants or State Bank loans. A redistribution of working capital envisaged in connection with economic reforms announced in the Soviet Union in the fall of 1965 underlines the basic identity of the two sources, for no interest is to be charged on loans that replace working capital formerly owned by enterprises and subsequently channeled elsewhere by higher echelon authorities. In regard to credit-financed fixed investment

---

[1] *In Hungary and East Germany an enterprise is not permitted to retain earnings to enlarge working capital.*

(which as mentioned is minor, except in agriculture), the link between budgetary resources and loans is quite direct, since the budget appropriates specified amounts to medium-term lending by the State Bank.[2]

In several countries, working capital judged to be in excess of needs is regularly siphoned off into the budget, through a combination of profit and turnover taxes, which is flexible enough to permit easy manipulation of working-capital funds left with any individual enterprise. The fact that enterprises have only limited authority over the use of their "own" working capital, as well as the always present possibility that this may be taken away ("redistributed") by the higher echelon authorities, encourages its wasteful use. There is therefore a strong incentive for enterprises to spend or conceal their working capital.

Thus no great significance can be attached to ratios showing the share of bank credit in working capital, or to the relation between credit volume and the value of aggregate output or any similar relationships. Since the division of working capital between "own" funds and credit is largely conventional—the result of administrative decision and manipulation, rather than a function of the profitability, growth rate, or creditworthiness of a given enterprise—quantitative analysis of credit use under the standard system has only limited analytical meaning. Moreover, the new policies now under way involve a reexamination of the role and distribution of "own" funds and credit in the working capital of enterprises.

With this word of warning, a few figures may be presented, in order to give a rough impression of magnitudes. Since 1950, bank credit in the Soviet Union has averaged over 40 per cent of the working capital in all nonagricultural segments of the economy (nearly 46 per cent at the end of 1964). The proportion is lower in the other countries, usually around 25 or 30 per cent, though in recent years there has been a tendency toward increasing the share of credit in the working capital of socialized enterprises. In the socialized sector of the communist coun-

---

[2] *The history of banking in Eastern Europe abounds with examples illustrating that the two types of financing have the same ultimate source and that any existing arrangements are rooted more in accounting convenience than in matters of substance. Thus, in Poland, bank loans made available in the first postwar years to finance investment in the socialized sector were subsequently transformed into grants, and a corresponding amount of government deposits on the balance sheet of the State Bank was wiped out. To cite a more recent example, at the beginning of 1965, State Bank loans to collective farms amounting to over 2 billion rubles were canceled in the Soviet Union, again with the cumulative budget surplus on deposit with the State Bank being reduced by an equivalent amount (in this instance, the loans had originally been made to finance working capital as well as fixed investment); housing loans made to veterans prior to 1947 were canceled in a similar way in 1965. The recent shifting from a grant to a loan basis in the financing of the bulk of capital investment, discussed in Chapter 8, underlines the point made here.*

tries the largest use of credit, in relation to average working-capital needs, is made by procurement agencies, including those that purchase the output of cooperative and individual farms; manufacturing makes the smallest use. Credit usually accounts for around two thirds of the working capital of retail trade.

Even before the initiation of the new policies there was a tendency to reduce the proportion of credit allocated to retail trade, in order to make more resources available to industry and agriculture; nevertheless, retail trade still accounts for the bulk of short-term credit, and its share has undergone little change over recent years, or even in the long run. The service industries have been neglected in all the countries ever since official banks became the sole source of credit. The low priority given these industries has contributed to glaring deficiencies in their entire range, from maintenance and repair to personal services. Although credit extended to the service sector is still, by and large, a negligible part of banking, the area may be expected to grow, judging from recent trends in public discussion.

In comparison with short-term financing of the state-owned sector, all other types of credit are considerably less important. Although in most of the countries agriculture is still the most important single economic sector, the amount of credit, both long and short term, made available to it by the banking system is relatively small. Long- term credit is extended to collective farms and independent farmers, where they have survived in significant numbers, to supplement their own resources for investment in farm equipment and livestock. The need for investment funds in agriculture is increased by the relatively backward farm technology that still characterizes these economies. Short-term lending to independent farmers and to farm cooperatives is usually geared to the cash outlays needed for seasonal production and to the amount of produce sold to state agencies in charge of purchasing farm output for urban consumption and export. Since each collective farm is an independent entity, its working funds do not benefit from infusions or reallocations by higher echelon units, and bank credit is the only means of overcoming any shortage of working capital, including normal seasonal needs; in the Soviet Union, 85 per cent of nonlabor inputs were met from bank loans in 1964.

The credit available to the private sector in industry and trade is an altogether insignificant part of total credit extended. The remaining privately owned enterprises are subject to discrimination in favor of the socialized sector, and in fact the power to extend or not to extend credit was widely used in the years of transition after the war as a means of reducing the sphere of private entrepreneurship. Particularly in Bulgaria and Rumania the extension of business credits to private individuals engaged in industry, commerce, or agriculture was severely restricted at the beginning of the communist rule. In East Germany, Poland, and Czechoslovakia, private entrepreneurs fared somewhat better and continued to receive limited amounts of credit from official banks after the nationalization of all large-scale industry. Private firms in these comparatively developed countries have helped to overcome shortages of some critically needed manufactured products.

The State Bank does not extend direct credit to the national government, either by acquiring securities or otherwise, though some indirect financing of government occurs when the bank provides credit to enterprises to permit them to effectuate payments into the budget. To the extent of such financing, budgetary surpluses, typically shown by all countries of Eastern Europe, are in effect the counterpart of bank loans. Bank credit is generally available to finance service establishments operated by municipal governments.

The use of credit has been widened since the mid-1950's. In recent years the communist countries have begun to use credit to stimulate technological progress and efficiency, to finance additional facilities for the production of consumer goods (mostly soft goods, usually referred to as "articles of mass consumption"), to provide public eating facilities and a variety of services (mostly personal and entertainment), and to finance consumer purchases and housing construction by individuals and cooperatives. On the whole, however, these credit uses are still minor. Medium-term credit to enterprises, which represented a first step toward credit financing of nonagricultural investment, accounts for only a small part of total credit outstanding; it is discussed in a separate section of this chapter. And the amount of credit available for consumer purchases and homeownership (see Chapter 6) is still limited, as judged by Western standards.

Such changes in the allocation of credit as have occurred in the various countries have resulted from administrative decisions, embodied in financial plans, rather than achieved by application of the monetary tools typically used by the central banks of the noncommunist countries. Under the standard system, interest is merely a service charge intended to meet operating costs, and rates tend to be uniform for all loans, irrespective of purpose. The low level of rates reflects the doctrinaire view that interest has no place in a socialist economy and that it is tainted by similarity to a particularly objectionable type of "parasite income" in capitalist countries. Even the use of greater differentiation of interest rates, which has become a general policy since the mid-1950's, merely reflects judgments as to how the cost of credit should be related to costs of products and distribution. It is not designed to influence the use of credit—a question that is settled by the plan.

SHORT-TERM CREDIT TO ENTERPRISES

Of the credit extended by all official banking institutions, including the specialized banks, short-term lending accounts for the overwhelming proportion. In the Soviet Union, for instance, the proportion at the end of 1950 was 86 per cent, and at the end of 1964 it had risen to 91 per cent. The lion's share of short-term credit is provided by the State Bank for the needs of the socialized sector of the economy. Short-term lending by the other official banks is geared to the special needs of the activities they service—agriculture, construction, and foreign trade— and follows, with proper modifications, the same general principles as that of the State Bank.

The bulk of short-term credit to enterprises is extended for the financing of inventories. As a rule, "own" funds are set and maintained at levels estimated as adequate to carry a fixed part (in some cases, all) of the normal stock of raw and semifinished materials and of goods in process required to achieve planned production goals; the remainder of normal inventories is carried on credit. The precise proportion of inventory to be credit financed is stipulated for each industry (often in great detail for individual types of raw and auxiliary materials) by higher level administrative authorities, with proper provision for seasonal variations, where appropriate. The setting and modification of these "norms" are used as a means of achieving specific operating goals, such as a decrease in the inventory-output ratio or a maximum degree of administrative control over the activities of individual enterprises, and much of the discussion on credit policy is concerned with their proper level. One of the important recent developments in most Eastern European countries has been a backing-away from excessive details and rigidity in setting these norms. In fact, Poland and Czechoslovakia have now given enterprises the right to determine their own norms.

Although the norms determine the volume of planned inventory credit, additional credit needs, not stipulated in the plan, arise whenever there are disruptions in the planned flow of materials and finished products. For instance, an inventory consisting of an almost finished locomotive must be financed if a supplier fails to deliver the whistle cord on time, whether the plan provided for such credit or not. Disruptions occur for a great variety of reasons: failure to receive parts or materials, because of transportation delays or plant breakdowns or whatever;

delivery of materials on or ahead of schedule to a plant producing below planned levels; nonavailability of railroad freight cars or other shipping facilities; even a change in the production plan after the needed raw materials have been received and paid for. (Frequent changes of plans are among the most criticized aspects of economic policy, and their elimination is one of the purposes of the reforms now being introduced.) Thus credits for unplanned purposes must also be provided for in the plan. They are intended to replenish working capital depleted by developments for which an enterprise is not directly responsible, especially to finance unforeseen accumulations of stocks.

Just as the rate at which planned credit is being drawn down indicates to the bank whether accumulation of inventory (and other activities) is proceeding according to plan, demands for additional accommodation signal trouble. Unplanned credits are likely to be granted if they will serve the interest of plan fulfillment or overfulfillment. They are generally refused if the enterprise has a poor performance record, or if the bank believes they would be used for accumulating abnormally large raw material inventories as a precaution against failure in the distribution system or for stockpiling goods that are of inferior quality or that are for any other reason unsalable.

Two basic types of inventory loans are made: one is geared to the *level* of stocks and the other to the *flow* of goods ("turnover"). Credit geared to the level of inventories, which was the predominant form through the early fifties, involves a separate application for each loan and is granted up to a "limit" set for each enterprise (comparable to a credit line granted by commercial banks in the West). The alternative method—gearing credit to output—was first tried in the Soviet Union in 1936. Hitherto the provision that only seasonal swings could be financed through bank credit had prevented enterprises from obtaining loans that would enable them to pay promptly for materials delivered ahead of schedule; their own free balances were insufficient for this purpose and could not be replenished until delivery of goods in process of production. (And in heavy industry even the provision for seasonal swings in inventory was very limited, in contrast to the food and other industries that use agricultural raw materials.) The logical development was to make credit available to finance the entire flow of materials through production. In effect, this involves an automatic extension of credit, under a continuous arrangement, to finance a stipulated proportion of all stocks carried by the enterprise (see page 116).

After their initiation in 1936, loans geared to turnover made very little headway in the Soviet Union until 1957, but in recent years they have accounted for

70 to 80 per cent of all short-term inventory credit in that country. Such loans were originally available only to designated industries, like those processing products of agriculture and forestry, and to procurement and trade organizations, but now they are also made to machine-building and other heavy industries. Financing of turnover has become the predominant form of credit in the other countries as well. Its popularity derives not only from its relative simplicity from an operating point of view, but also from the fact that it permits more effective and meaningful control of the performance of each enterprise.

In line with the basic philosophy that goods should move rapidly to the next stage of production and distribution, there are strong efforts to prevent over-accumulation of inventories. Continuous admonitions and pressures by the State Bank and by the economic and even the political authorities attempt to combat protective hoarding and slackness in completing production, which slow down the flow of goods to final consumers. Indeed, reduction of inventory-output (or sales) ratios has been one of the more permanent goals of economic policy in all countries of Eastern Europe, and the State Bank is expected to play a leading role in this never-ending struggle, even though determination of the "proper" level of aggregate inventories lies beyond its authority. Pressure to reduce inventories can be exercised most successfully in the area of distribution, since here the need for assuring adequate supplies of raw materials, fuel, and other necessities and problems arising from imbalance in the flow of components, about which the State Bank can do little, are not relevant.

Despite the bank's efforts—and despite the all-encompassing planning and the absence of cyclical fluctuations—chronic overaccumulation of inventories plagues all communist economies, more severely at some times than at others. One factor seems to be the excessive geographic centralization of supply organizations, which results in a large amount of cross-hauling (particularly in the Soviet Union), thus augmenting the volume of goods in transit. The "speculative" motive rooted in expectations of price changes is not present in a system where prices are fixed by administrative decision and changed infrequently. However, there is a general tendency to protect operations from supply and transportation bottlenecks by hoarding raw materials, and this is encouraged by the low cost and semiautomatic character of credit. In addition, production bottlenecks and unbalanced inventories of raw materials result in a damming-up of goods in process. Finally, because of lack of market guidance, inventories of finished consumer goods tend to be high and include a large proportion of wrong sizes and models not in demand. In recent years this problem has been aggravated by consumers' rejection of goods of poor quality and unfashionable design.

Credit policy has recently been used quite generally to achieve a greater responsiveness to consumer preferences. Banks have sought to induce retail trade organizations to reduce or liquidate low-quality inventories (if necessary, by cutting prices), and their persuasion has used means not unknown in the rest of the world, such as refusal to renew loans or renewing them at significantly higher rates. Thus in 1959 restrictive measures were introduced in the Soviet Union against trade organizations that accumulate finished products for which there is insufficient or no demand; a year later, provision was made for the extension of special credits to trade organizations that take losses by marking down prices of goods which have become outmoded or whose quality has deteriorated.

After inventory financing, the next main use of short-term credit is for bridging the collection gap. Loans are granted for the period—usually short—during which payments documents are in the process of collection. The system amounts to an automatic financing of all accounts receivable, thus restoring the working capital of the seller without putting additional pressure on the buyer to discharge his obligation promptly. There is considerable indebtedness of this kind; in the period from 1950 to 1963, accounts receivable ranged between 12 per cent and 20 per cent of the current assets of Soviet enterprises.

This system of accounts receivable financing differs from direct interenterprise indebtedness—which is banned—not only because it uses the bank as inter- mediary but also because the indebtedness arises at the initiative of the buyer, who delays payments, and is not a device employed by sellers to stimulate sales. Such a system is bound to benefit the careless or ill-intentioned debtor at the expense of the creditor, who may find himself unable to repay the credit within the normal collection period for which it was granted. This has finally been recognized, at least in the Soviet Union, where changes announced in the fall of 1965 shift the burden of financing the transfer gap to the buyer, who will now have to obtain bank credit to pay his bills on time.

Further financing needs have nothing to do with the "movement of real assets", but arise from the peculiar accounting arrangements that are a feature of communist economies. For instance, in each accounting period, which may be as short as five or ten days, the proportion of profits that the given enterprise is supposed to achieve in that period (according to planned, not actual, costs) is automatically paid into the national budget. If such profit has not actually been earned in the period, the resulting depletion of working capital may have to be offset by a bank loan. After the end of the month, when the actual profit has been determined, adjustments must be made all along the line. This is merely one example of "borrowing to fulfill the financial plan", which is mainly a means of exerting administrative control through credit relations, at considerable cost in accounting and verification time.

As was discussed in the first section of this chapter, the original requirement that financing be specific involved compartmentalization of loans by purpose, with a rigid definition of the purposes that were permissible. Gradually, new "objects of crediting" were added, and the number of separate loan categories multiplied, but for each newly eligible "object" there was still detailed stipulation of the conditions under which the loan could be obtained, and of the mode of repayment. Credit could not be extended unless its purpose was specifically mentioned on the approved list. Actually, of course, the rigor of logic was frequently circumvented by the necessities of practice, and thus—in addition to the categories of loans that neatly fitted the planned movement of goods—various categories of "transitional", "special", "interim", and "extraordinary" credit were introduced (all four terms were actually in use in Poland in the early fifties). Basically, there was no alternative to providing such funds, if a chain reaction was to be avoided; whether they were provided under special headings or merely charged to an overdue credit account mattered little. The fact of the matter is that the high principles and elaborate procedures of "socialist credit" required automatic extension of credit to validate any distortion, whether it resulted from uncontrollable causes, administrative failures, misjudgment in planning, or mismanagement of real resources.

The proliferation of separate loan categories entailed frequent transfers by the State Bank among the several accounts (clearing and loan) that each enterprise maintained at a given bank branch. Details varied for individual industries or branches of trade, but they uniformly involved numerous book entries and served the general purpose of providing maximum State Bank control over the flow of payments in order to assure repayment. Thus the keeping of separate loan accounts increased the burden on the bank, and the addition of new "objects of crediting" continuously added to the details of required current statistical reporting. There was a continuing search for the best method, given the specific conditions of the industry, of assuring the retirement of each loan from the flow of receipts generated by sales. This involved frequent changes of procedure, which usually resulted in more paper work and more administrative controls.

Doubts about the effectiveness of the whole area of credit administration became so widespread that by the late fifties all the Eastern European countries had begun to abandon the belief that the end use of credit could be controlled by extending credit for authorized purposes only. Since the end of the Stalin era there has been a gradual breaking-away from the view that, in order to preserve monetary equilibrium, the extension of credit should be limited to the financing of identifiable real assets. What began as a cautious exploration of possibilities for introducing greater flexibility in the granting of credit to encourage initiative and efficiency led to a successive broadening of the interpretation of the five principles of socialist credit to encompass almost all types of working-capital needs known in capitalist countries.

Granting of credit for broader purposes, including general working-capital loans, rather than for specific needs was introduced in the Soviet Union in 1954, and a little later in the other countries, with a simultaneous liberalization of credit terms. Thus the number of separate purposes for which loans could be obtained was reduced in Poland from twenty to seven and in Rumania from more than thirteen to eight. Gradually the Soviet Union began to simplify accounting by merging the various special loan accounts and channeling receipts more directly into loan repayment transactions. The consolidation of subaccounts has since made considerable progress in the Soviet Union. Logically, its ultimate outcome would be the complete consolidation of the current and the separate loan accounts into a single account for each enterprise. This would facilitate analysis of the proper use of a given unit's working capital and its overall need for bank financing. Proposals along these lines are currently under discussion in the Soviet Union. Hungary has pioneered in this area, shifting away from the practice of tying all loans to specific purposes and collateral by introducing, in 1957, a "single production credit", secured by all real assets of the given enterprise rather than by specific categories of inventory.

Flexibility of credit administration has been greatly increased, particularly since the late fifties, by authorizing bank offices to transfer unused credit quotas among territories and among enterprises of the same industry. Also, a certain proportion of planned credits (in the Soviet Union, 5 per cent of the total volume earmarked for any major geographic area or ministry) is placed in an unassigned fund, from which loans are made to enterprises that perform exceptionally well.

Another important aspect of the recent developments has been the preferential treatment accorded to "good" performers. The principle of systematic differentiation depending on performance was introduced in the Soviet Union in 1954, at the same time that credit sanctions applicable to poor performers were tightened (see the following section). Successful enterprises are now able to obtain credit on favorable terms to meet contingencies that arise through no fault of their own. Such "unplanned credits" were described above in connection with inventory financing. This differential granting of additional credit facilities involves assessment of the quality of an enterprise's performance. Efficiency is generally measured in terms of meeting the physical targets of production plans, and success in maintaining the planned levels of costs per unit of output and in achieving increases in labor productivity in accordance with the previously set targets.

With the notable exception of the Soviet Union, the recent trend has been generally toward downgrading details in credit plans to the status of guidelines, and toward permitting local branch managers greater freedom in dealing with loan applications. The increased basing of interenterprise relations on contracts, rather than on plans imposed from above, has contributed to enlarging the role of local bank officials and to making the extension of credit dependent on the state of order books rather than on plan targets. By now, the notion that credit must follow trade has been discarded in practice, and the semiautomatic crediting on the basis of plans has been largely done away with.

CREDIT SANCTIONS

The State Bank of a communist country can hardly acquire bad assets, since with few exceptions (such as lending to farm cooperatives and individuals) a higher echelon organization can be asked to guarantee the credit granted and to take remedial action to improve the performance of the borrower. But the assets the State Bank acquires can be slow, and the volume of overdue loans, resulting mainly from the inability to control inventories, has been a continuous problem in all countries of Eastern Europe. The need to reduce the volume of overdue loans is a recurrent theme in the financial periodicals and official statements.

Under the standard system, direct administrative measures—those available to the State Bank (and the specialized banks) and those requiring appeal to the higher echelon economic authorities—constitute the main means for remedial action. The disciplinary measures applied directly by the official banks are known as "credit sanctions"; they are applied to assure fulfillment of the economic plan, and not primarily to safeguard the interest of the bank as a lender. With regard both to loans and to current (clearing) accounts, the State Bank is in a position to apply such sanctions promptly and directly, even though measures for remedying the underlying situation must be initiated by political authorities and by the administration that supervises the operations of a given enterprise.

The principle of credit sanctions had already been established in the Soviet Union at the time of the credit reforms of 1930-32, and the subsequent development of this tool has a rich history. The scope of controls by the Gosbank was widened significantly in 1954, when that institution was made responsible for evaluating the success of the individual enterprise in fulfilling its economic plan with regard to capital formation, reduction of unit costs, and protection of working capital. Between 1955 and 1957, credit sanctions were introduced in the other countries.

One generally used sanction is to put poor performers on a special regime, which typically involves increased control pressure to liquidate excessive inventories or to complete production held up for lack of parts, and enforcement of a rigid system of priorities over payments. In some cases the bank may require, for future loans, a guarantee of the higher echelon authority (for instance, the ministry to which the enterprise is subordinated or the local authorities who supervise the enterprise), but apparently there are few cases where the guarantor actually has to make good on the obligations of the enterprise; more frequently, he takes direct administrative action to improve its performance.

Penalty rates for overdue loans are another generally used form of credit sanctions. Such loans are placed by banks in a special category, and interest rates on renewals are sharply increased from the original nominal levels, reaching as high as 7 per cent in Bulgaria, 10.8 per cent in Czechoslovakia, 12 per cent in Poland, and even 18 per cent in East Germany and Hungary. High interest rates are particularly effective in trade, where bank credit constitutes a substantial proportion of working capital and interest payments represent a comparatively large part of total costs.

More extreme measures involve suspension of access to the more liberal (or less controllable) forms of credit, the taking-over of collateral (goods), complete withdrawal of all credit facilities, and as a last resort forced sale of the collateral and ultimate declaration of bankruptcy.[3]

---

[3] See N. S. Malein, Kreditno-raschetnye pravootnosheniia i finansovyi kontrol' (Legal Relations Concerning Credit and Settlements and Financial Control), Moscow, 1964, pages 113-22.

Short of such extreme measures, credit sanctions, particularly the charging of penalty rates, have proved largely ineffective. Payment of interest, even at penalty rates for overdue loans, is clearly not much of an inhibiting factor under a system based on the fulfillment of physical production goals and other "real" criteria, with management having only a limited concern with the size of profits. In the last analysis the cost of increased interest is borne by the national budget and does not directly affect either the most relevant success indicators (in terms of physical magnitudes) or the income of management. In the new policies now being worked out, some of the first steps include making penalty payments affect the compensation of managers and the fringe benefits of the staff.

CREDIT FOR FIXED INVESTMENT

In spite of the scant significance of credit for the financing of plant and equipment in the state-owned sector, the experience gained through the use of this technique since the midfifties has no doubt contributed to the shift from grant to loan financing now taking place to varying degrees in the different countries. Investment loans are now made in all the countries, at terms of up to three and apparently even to six or more years. Actually, these should be regarded as medium-term loans, but they are included with short-term credit, at least in Soviet statistics, probably because in practice they are amortized quite rapidly (in the Soviet Union, within little over one year, on the average). In fact, they were originally made available only for purposes profitable enough to permit relatively quick retirement.

The specific purposes for which such investment loans can be granted vary among countries, but they invariably fall within certain broad categories: acquisition of machinery or equipment embodying advanced technology (including automated equipment); acquisition of equipment for which, for one reason or another, no provision was made in the plan ("afterthought projects"); or an increase in the output of consumption goods, mainly on the basis of locally available raw materials or by-products. In principle, the investment to be financed must improve technology, rather than break bottlenecks; one frequently heard complaint is that under these provisions one can buy, for instance, an automatic lathe, but not build another freight elevator which would cut costs by a much larger amount.

Most of the loans are for projects not included in the national investment plans—that is, either for small technological improvements or for "decentralized" (not centrally planned) investment, which except in the Soviet Union has now become a significant part of investment in the socialized sector. Stringent requirements are attached to such loans, primarily to prevent consummation of projects which were excluded from the investment plan because they were rejected by the higher echelon economic and planning authorities. An example is the provision that construction cannot exceed a small part of the proposed investment (not more than 15 per cent in the Soviet Union and Rumania).

In Czechoslovakia, credit for small technological improvements was introduced in 1954 (with a maximum maturity of two to three years), but remained of very limited significance until 1959 when the scope of loan financing was widened to include "decentralized investment" not provided for in the central plan. Enterprises' unspent funds for amortization and other investment purposes, which were previously returned to the budget at the end of each year, are now being left with the State Bank to form a fund for these decentralized investment loans, which have terms as long as six years. Since 1959, loan financing, as an alternative to grants, has been available even for investment projects included in the central plan. Indeed, Czechoslovakia and Poland were probably the first countries of Eastern Europe to make a significant move toward putting the financing of fixed capital investment in the state sector on a repayable loan basis. In Poland, credit for technological improvements was introduced in 1955, with maturity up to one year, and loans for unplanned decentralized investment were made possible in 1958, for maximum terms of five or possibly even ten years.

"Loans for small mechanization" were initiated in the Soviet Union as early as 1932, but the numerous restrictions attached to them prevented such lending from attaining much importance. Even after the provisions governing the extension of such loans were liberalized, the changes failed to result in any appreciable growth during the Stalin era, and at the end of 1954 the total of such loans outstanding was only 20 million rubles.[4] After a further liberalization in 1954, the amounts outstanding began increasing. In recent years, the Soviet Union, following the lead of Czechoslovakia and Hungary, broadened the use of loans for technical improvements and for enlarging the output of mass consumption goods. During 1964, loans extended for small mechanization amounted to 552 million rubles and loans for augmenting production facilities for articles of mass con-

---

[4] *For a detailed discussion of these loans, see Gregory Grossman, "Gold and the Sword: Money in the Soviet Command Economy"*, Industrialization in Two Systems: Essays in Honor of Alexander Gerschenkron, *edited by Henry Rosovsky (New York: John Wiley & Sons, Inc., 1966).*

sumption came to 354 million rubles. Over the five-year period 1960-64, about one third of the amount of loans in this general category was for automation and mechanization, one third for the acquisition or replacement of equipment, and the remaining third for all other purposes, including the introduction of new technology.[5] These statistics show that, in comparison with 38.7 billion rubles of total fixed investment in industry made in 1964 alone, this type of credit financing plays a rather meager role.

In Rumania, modernization credits (with a maturity of up to three years) were introduced in 1954, as were also credits for financing investments designed to use by-products of industry or to increase the output of articles for mass consumption. Credit for small mechanization has been widely used there— perhaps more generally than in the other countries—and, contrary to the general rule, it can be used to break production bottlenecks. Under this heading, loans have been made to enlarge the output of basic raw materials (such as caustic soda) and for import substitution. The number of individual small mechanization loans has been increasing rapidly, rising from 309 in 1954 to about 7,900 in 1963. In 1957 the conditions governing such credits were liberalized. Further steps in this direction were taken in 1963, when maximum limits for single loans were raised and the interest rate was lowered, with an increase of the bank's role in examining the effectiveness of proposed investment.

Also in East Germany, medium-term credit financing is used essentially for projects involving modernization of equipment; in the years 1956-60 it was a considerably more important source of total investment funds there than in the Soviet Union. East Germany, too, has relaxed the requirements with regard to very short recoupment periods and high rates of profits required on loan-financed investments.

Despite the recent increase in some countries, the growth of modernization loans has been slow. An important reason is that there is little inducement to borrow, even at nominal interest cost, as long as the enterprise can obtain investment funds free, on a nonreturnable basis (though perhaps only next year or later), by having the project included in the regular investment plan. Further reasons are the delays in obtaining such loans and the difficulties in acquiring materials and machinery from the authorities in charge of allocations. Their use is likely to

---

[5] *N. Barkovskii, "Credit Financing of Capital Formation", D. K., July 1965, page 5.*

become more general, however, with the introduction of a charge for the use of investment and working-capital funds allocated to individual enterprises from budgetary resources and as a result of the general shift to loan financing and from centralized allocation of all material resources and outputs to contracting between the interested parties.

6. Banking Facilities for the Nonsocialized Sector

In contrast to the preceding chapters, which have dealt with the financing, servicing, and control of the socialized sector by the monobank and the specialized banks, this chapter is concerned with the saving and borrowing transactions of the population and the nonsocialized sector of the economy. These transactions are typically carried out through a single nationwide savings bank system, but the arrangements for them are considerably less uniform than those in the socialized sector. In the consumer area the Soviet Union did not play the universal role of a prototype, and thus the specific arrangements and policies now pursued in the various countries have in many cases no precedent in Soviet experience. Shaped to a certain extent by pre-World War II experience and traditions, they differ considerably from country to country and are on the whole more imaginative and flexible than those in the Soviet Union.

Although in general the savings bank system services the population while the monobank services the socialized sector, this division of activities is not entirely clear-cut. In the Soviet Union the Gosbank rather than the savings bank system makes direct loans for home construction and also finances the retail trade network, which extends credit to consumers; and in Bulgaria consumers obtain retail credit from retail stores but mortgage loans from the Investment Bank. In all the other countries, both consumer banking and home financing are the province of the savings bank system, shared in some instances with organizations resembling our credit unions, which operate as agencies of the savings bank in factories, state farms, and various other places of employment. Except in the Soviet Union the savings banks and credit cooperatives (and even the monobank) extend some credit to private or cooperative entrepreneurship, in order to accommodate the small but in many respects important sector of the economy that provides the population with services and some goods that the socialized enterprises are unable or unwilling to supply; this sector accounts for a significant part of agricultural output even where the overwhelming bulk of farm land is collectivized. In some countries the savings banks make a small amount of credit available to the socialized sector, through loans to finance facilities constructed by the lower units of government.

STRUCTURE AND ACTIVITIES OF SAVINGS BANKS

In the countries of Eastern Europe the nationwide savings bank system is not only the single general-purpose savings institution but usually the only banking facility available to the population, since the State Bank and the specialized banks normally do not deal with individuals. Even where savings accounts can be opened with credit institutions that extend loans to the nonsocialized sector, such as artisan banks and farm credit cooperatives, the bulk of the population's savings (80-85 per cent) is with the national savings bank system. In several countries this system is also the main or sole source of consumer credit. In the Soviet Union and Bulgaria, however, all funds collected by the savings bank system are redeposited with the State Bank. Even in the other countries, savings deposits not used for lending are redeposited with the State Bank or with the Treasury, and become part of the pool from which loans are made to the socialized sector of the economy.

Savings bank accounts may be owned not only by physical persons but also by nonprofit organizations, collective farms, and the lowest level municipal entities (such as villages). In general, current accounts that are not important enough to require concentration in the State Bank for the purpose of planning and control, including some from the socialized sector, are carried in savings banks. In the Soviet Union, for instance, these banks handle accounts for hospitals, children's homes and camps, administrations of municipally owned housing, mutual aid societies, trade union branches, and various voluntary associations; in localities where there is no convenient office of the Gosbank they also carry accounts of collective farms.

The savings bank system developed in some countries from an existing postal savings system. At present a separate postal savings bank survives only in East Germany but, in some countries, agencies of the savings bank system operate in post and telegraph offices. In the Soviet Union, for instance, three fourths of the entire savings network consists of such offices, operated on a part-time basis by the regular employees of the postal administration, who receive additional compensation from the savings bank. As a rule, the savings network maintains considerably more cashier's windows than the State Bank.

Normally the savings bank system is supervised by the Ministry of Finance, usually as part of a division that is also responsible for the placement of government bonds with the population. In the Soviet Union, however, the network of savings banks was transferred on January 1, 1963 from the Ministry of Finance to the Gosbank, and in Rumania savings banks have always been subordinated to the State Bank.

The services provided by savings banks are much more limited than those available to individuals from commercial banks and savings institutions in Western countries. In addition to offering a variety of savings accounts (described in the following section), they provide limited facilities for the transfer of funds; a depositor can usually instruct the bank to make payments for rent, utilities, and taxes. In most countries, savings banks issue money orders that are cashable at other offices and thus fulfill the function of traveler's checks; a similar purpose is served by passbooks from which limited withdrawals may be made at any office. Savings banks also sell and redeem government savings bonds (only Hungary and Bulgaria have discontinued their sale), service them (pay coupons and lottery prizes, provide safekeeping facilities), and in some countries (including the Soviet Union) buy obligations before maturity, on demand. They also sell tickets for national or regional lotteries and distribute the winning prizes. Savings banks may make certain payments on behalf of the government or its institutions; in the Soviet Union, for instance, they pay out old-age pensions and various social security benefits, such as aid to large families and dependent children.

In the various communist countries the structure and activities of consumer savings and credit institutions reflect a variety of historical factors and traditions. The Soviet Union presents one extreme case. There, a single savings bank system, and that alone, provides savings facilities,[1] and it does not engage in lending. No cooperative credit organizations have survived. The central cooperative bank (Moscow Narodny Bank) was originally exempt from the wholesale nationaliza-

---

[1] *The Gosbank issues "deposit passbooks" to individuals for demand and time deposits, but these are of very limited significance, perhaps because a minimum deposit of 300 rubles is required. A separate passbook (actually a certificate) is issued for each demand deposit; for time deposits no more than three separate deposits are permissible in one passbook.*

tion of banks, but in 1918 it was absorbed by the predecessor of the Gosbank. Several organizations to provide credit to producer and consumer cooperatives were created during the twenties, but all were liquidated by 1930, at the time of the collectivization drive. Poland and East Germany are at the other end of the spectrum, having adapted a number of previously existing institutions to play a part in servicing consumers.

PERSONAL SAVINGS

In most Eastern European countries the number of savings accounts is very large in relation to the total population (in Czechoslovakia there are nine pass-books for every ten inhabitants), but average *per capita* savings are small, ranging (at so-called "noncommercial" exchange rates) from less than $100 in the Soviet Union, Poland, and Hungary to over $300 in East Germany. Five basic types of accounts are offered: regular passbook accounts from which withdrawals can be made on demand, those that can be withdrawn at maturity (with the minimum maturity ranging from three months in Hungary to twelve months in Poland), checking accounts, special accounts (in the name of a child, for instance, and payable at completion of school), and lottery accounts.[2]

Lottery accounts draw no interest, the earnings being distributed in the form of prizes (ranging from 10 per cent to 250 per cent) proportionate to the balance at the time of the drawing. In Czechoslovakia more than 42 per cent of savings bank deposits are in lottery accounts. In Poland such accounts (representing about 16 per cent of all savings deposits) entitle the holders to participate in drawings for durable goods (such as automobiles and motorcycles) or fully paid vacation trips. (Lotteries for cash or merchandise prizes—amounting to only 20 per cent of the funds raised—were conducted in the Soviet Union during the war for the benefit of the Treasury; since 1958 they have been operated by the individual federated republics, the prizes consisting of houses, cars, appliances, watches, and so on, and representing 50 per cent of the value of the tickets sold.) In Bulgaria, too, savers can open accounts that enable them to participate in mixed cash and merchandise lotteries. The savings banks offer checking ("current") accounts in the Soviet Union, Poland, and East Germany, and in the

[2] *V. Bochkova and D. Butakov, "Savings of the Population and the Way in Which They are Attracted in the European Countries of People's Democracy", D. K., March 1965.*

latter country they operate a giro-transfer system similar to that of several countries of Western Europe. In addition to passbooks in the name of the holder, some countries (Czechoslovakia, Hungary, East Germany) offer "bearer accounts" identified only by a number.

Encouragement of personal savings has been much emphasized in recent years in the communist countries, where it is regarded as an important means of avoiding excess consumer demand, given the chronic shortage of consumer goods, and as a means of raising the level of the population's material well-being. The volume of savings has risen sharply, stimulated first by the discontinuance of the more or less forced placement of government bonds with the population and then, in recent years, by the increase in incomes, the greater availability of durable goods, and the official encouragement of privately and cooperatively financed housing construction. The bulk of personal savings is of a temporary nature, the funds being accumulated to buy specific but relatively expensive items (which may be just a winter coat or a motorcycle) or to undertake a vacation trip.[3] An important factor in the growth of savings deposits was that such deposits were uniformly given a preferential rate at the time of the various currency conversions and monetary reforms.

Saving is promoted in a variety of ways. Wage earners are encouraged to have their pay deposited directly in savings accounts (Soviet Union), and farm cooperatives (in Czechoslovakia) are urged to deposit in such accounts all cash payments due their members. Regular (contractual) saving is encouraged (Czechoslovakia, Hungary), and special accounts for children (Bulgaria) and teen-agers (Hungary) are promoted. In recent years, some countries have introduced special-purpose accounts whose owners have priority claims for the purchase of goods in short supply (cars, for instance, in Poland). Accounts specifically for the accumulation of downpayments on houses and apartments are made available in several countries; in Poland the holder even obtains a guarantee that, if building costs rise, the savings bank will make good the difference between the actual cost and that stipulated in the savings contract. In East Germany, savings accounts and interest income from them are exempt from inheritance and income taxes; similar fiscal inducements may exist elsewhere.

---

[3] *The* Finansovo-Kreditnyi Slovar' *(Dictionary of Finance and Credit), 2 vols., Moscow, 1961 and 1964, states that under socialism "savings are intended mainly to meet various large expenditures— durable goods, vacation trips, etc." (Vol. II, page 323).*

East Germany and Rumania (since 1958) permit the savings banks to attract savings by issuing their own obligations. In East Germany these are sold to increase the resources available for financing residential construction, and are patterned after mortgage bonds (*Hypothekenpfandbriefe*) that have been widely used in Germany for centuries; such obligations are issued (since 1954) also by the Investment Bank, and both varieties may be purchased at any banking institution. They are in bearer form, freely transferable, and acceptable as loan collateral.

Interest rates on savings deposits are now quite generally differentiated in favor of the longest maturities or withdrawal-notice periods. Accounts from which withdrawals are permitted without notice draw from 2 per cent in Czechoslovakia and the Soviet Union to 5 per cent in Rumania, with 3 per cent being the prevailing rate elsewhere.

CONSUMER CREDIT

Short-term credit for the purchase of consumer goods is now generally available to the population. Because of the shortage of consumer goods the need for such credit did not arise during the first four decades of the Soviet regime, or until recent years in any of the other Eastern European countries. The need developed, however, as the income of a significant segment of the population rose above the subsistence level and as a more ample supply of consumer goods became available. This stage was reached in the countries neighboring the Soviet Union about ten years after World War II, in the Soviet Union somewhat later.[4]

Methods of financing consumer purchases vary. In Rumania, credit is extended by the State Bank to retail stores (at 4 per cent), which in turn accommodate consumers (at 6 per cent), and this principle is followed also in some other countries. In the Soviet Union, where consumer credit was introduced in the late fifties, the employer deducts instalments from the pay envelope and remits them to the retail stores, but experiments with direct credit extension by retail stores are under way. Consumer credit in Poland is extended by savings banks, credit unions, or (in rural areas) credit cooperatives. Hungarian and Czechoslovak savings banks make consumer loans directly to the buyer, who

---

[4] *See Marshall I. Goldman, "The Reluctant Consumer"*, Journal of Political Economy, *August 1965.*

pays in cash and repays the loan in instalments. In some countries, goods in adequate or excessive supply are placed on lists of items eligible for consumer financing; these lists are changed from time to time and may not be the same in all parts of the country.

The types of goods sold on credit differ considerably from the patterns prevailing in Western countries, the most striking contrast being that in most countries automobiles—which are uniformly in short supply—are not sold on credit. Downpayments are larger, and maturities shorter, than in the United States. Interest rate charges range up to 9 per cent (in Hungary for eighteen-month loans). Penalties for overdue instalments are usually heavy. There is great variety among communist countries in the special types of consumer credit made available to the population. In Czechoslovakia special loans are available to the newly wed; in Hungary savings banks make loans for various large family expenditures, such as marriages or funerals, and to workers who have lost their jobs as a result of mechanization, improvements in productivity, factory reorganizations, and the like.

HOME FINANCING

Because of the inability of the authorities to solve the housing shortage—resulting from population growth, war destruction, the influx into the urban centers, inadequate supply of building materials for residential construction, poor maintenance of the existing stock, subsidized rent, and more recently the demands for better accommodations associated with rising real income—private and cooperative initiative in housing construction has been uniformly encouraged in recent years by loans with long maturities, low rates, and liberal repayment provisions. In some of the countries, private and cooperative housing construction already accounts for a significant and rising part of the additions to the housing stock. Some countries, following Western examples, are now attempting to link the availability of mortgage and personal housing credit to the savings efforts of individuals. Typically, extension of housing credit is linked to the borrower's accumulation of a substantial part of the purchase price in an earmarked account with the savings bank, which advances the balance once the stipulated amount has been accumulated.

Loans for housing construction (in some cases, unsecured personal as well as mortgage loans) are made to individuals and housing cooperatives by savings banks in Hungary, East Germany, and Czechoslovakia. In East Germany, for instance, financing is available for up to 75 per cent of the building costs of individual homes, with ½ of 1 per cent of the loan to be amortized each year. Long-term loans (also up to 75 per cent of the cost of construction) are made to building cooperatives; although these are administered by savings banks they are actually made from budgetary resources, and no interest is charged. Cooperatives and individuals may also obtain credit from the savings banks for the purchase of government-owned apartments and houses. Loans are usually available for the repair of war-damaged buildings, for alterations, and for purchase of building materials.

The terms of housing loans are typically generous, in order to channel the maximum amount of the consumers' income into residential construction; frequently the interest rate charged is lower than the rate paid on savings accounts. Social and political considerations enter in many ways into the financing of non-government residential construction. In Czechoslovakia, for instance, technicians willing to take jobs in rural communities receive preferential terms.

LOANS FOR PRODUCTION AND CAPITAL INVESTMENT

Credit to various kinds of urban production cooperatives, repair and artisan shops, and other small-scale private undertakings is usually extended by credit cooperatives, whose resources are constituted in part by purchased membership shares and in part by free funds accumulated by the members; in some countries these cooperatives extend to their members consumer and housing as well as production credit. The savings banks, too, make loans in some countries to small urban entrepreneurs and independent farmers, for equipment and inventory needs. (In Hungary, for instance, savings banks make credit available for the purchase of capital equipment and inventories by self-employed persons and such small entrepreneurs as shoemakers, tailors, barbers, or repairmen, and also extend credit to production cooperatives that operate repair, service, and trade establishments. In East Germany the savings banks make instalment loans to artisans and small businessmen, who keep their accounts with the banks and make all payments through them.) Similarly, the savings banks may make loans to members of farm cooperatives and to independent farmers, for the purchase of livestock, for production expenditures, and for the construction of farm buildings. Maturities may range up to fifteen years (for construction financing). Interest rates vary, depending on purpose, down to zero for loans to victims of natural disasters.

7. Foreign Operations

Foreign trade is of vital importance to the countries of Eastern Europe, though in this respect the Soviet Union is rather a special case. Its economy developed originally in a climate of isolation from the capitalist world, and its rich and diversified resources enabled it to continue less dependent on foreign trade than its neighbors. The other communist regimes took over economies that had developed as an integral part of Europe, and despite their subsequent hectic and costly efforts to develop intrabloc trade—particularly by drawing on the raw material resources of the Soviet Union—these countries continue to depend to a very significant degree on imports payable in Western currencies. Thus, by necessity, the foreign trade relations of the communist countries have developed into two separate though interrelated spheres: intrabloc trade, conducted largely on the basis of arbitrary and conventional accounting units and planned in the hope of achieving a better coordination of the various countries' industrialization efforts; and trade with the countries outside the bloc. Trade with the West is based on prices established in competitive world markets and generally is conducted in convertible currencies; trade with underdeveloped countries is transacted, in part, on the basis of bilateral clearing arrangements.

Foreign trade (and, to a lesser extent, the purchase of foreign services) is so essential to all the Eastern European countries that it has become a crucial part of national economic planning. Because of the need to husband exchange earnings to pay for essential imports, a monopoly of foreign trade and foreign exchange was an early and distinctive characteristic of the planned economies. At the same time, the pressing need to earn convertible exchange led to a divorcing of export from domestic prices (themselves frequently having only a tenuous relation to costs) and to production priorities that tended to aggravate the misallocation of domestic resources. This effect is now being gradually recognized in the communist countries, as their trade with the West develops and the artificiality of some of their intrabloc exchanges becomes more and more obvious. The stresses and strains, which are evident in their political relations and within the newly established International Bank for Economic Cooperation (IBEC), have led them to various efforts to reorient their foreign trade relations—efforts that in most of the countries are related also to a desire for greater national independence.

The entire foreign trade of the Eastern European countries—both among themselves and with other nations—is carried out by special state trading organizations which act as intermediaries between domestic enterprises and foreign firms. Until the reforms of recent years, direct dealings between domestic producers and foreign customers were banned, but in some countries the ban has now been relaxed in an effort to encourage exports and, to a more limited extent, to facilitate the purchase of foreign capital goods by enterprises anxious to acquire equipment of advanced design or technology. Developments along these lines have occurred in Czechoslovakia, Hungary, and more recently in Bulgaria. But such developments by no means change the basic principle of central planning and monopoly of all foreign trade and foreign exchange. In recent years, some countries have begun to encourage exports by leaving a specific amount of hard currency proceeds at the disposal of firms producing for export. A related new development is foreign exchange loans to enterprises producing for export, thereby enabling them to purchase machinery and equipment abroad that will increase export earnings. In Poland, for instance, a special fund for this purpose, administered by the Ministry of Foreign Trade, was established in 1963.

The management of the foreign exchange monopoly is relatively easy under the conditions inherent in a communist economy, in which all export and import activities are also a government monopoly and are concentrated in the hands of specialized organizations. All local producers of export goods and all those who require imports of raw materials and finished goods must conduct their transactions through these state trading organizations (usually subordinated to the Ministry of Foreign Trade), and all trade payments pass through them. In addition, there is strict control over foreign travel and even remittances from abroad, and only a limited range of nontrade transactions are permitted (most of which, such as transportation, insurance, and foreign travel, are also carried out by specialized government organizations). Thus the job of completely controlling the flow of foreign exchange presents few problems. The foreign exchange proceeds of export organizations are converted at official rates, and domestic suppliers are paid in national currency. Conversely, approval of imports (or service payments) automatically entails the right to obtain the required foreign exchange, which is placed at the disposal of the foreign trade organizations.

The bulk of the international payments of the Eastern European countries is amongst themselves. All their trade, credit, and payments agreements with one another use the ruble as a unit of account, and contracts between export and import organizations of these countries are expressed in rubles, as are also all prices (even when they are keyed to world market prices expressed in dollars or in sterling). Payments other than those arising from merchandise trade—for

95

tourism, various service transactions, and so on—are denominated in the currency of the country where the service has been rendered. These payments are cleared through separate "noncommercial" accounts, on the basis of exchange rates that differ from the official exchange rates by the amount of fixed premiums or discounts. Until 1964, both "commercial" and "noncommercial" payments were cleared through bilateral accounts maintained by the respective Foreign Trade or State Banks; now, all such accounts are cleared through the IBEC. Its operations are discussed in a separate section of this chapter.

The various countries' relations with international monetary institutions reflect differences in the political developments leading to the establishment of domination by the communist party. Czechoslovakia and Poland originally joined the International Monetary Fund and the International Bank for Reconstruction and Development, and withdrew only under Soviet pressure (the first in 1950, the second in 1954). On the other hand, those countries that joined the Bank for International Settlements before World War II—Czechoslovakia, Hungary, Poland, and Rumania—have maintained their membership.

FINANCING OF FOREIGN TRADE

Except in Rumania, all payments relating to foreign trade are now channeled through the Foreign Trade Banks, which hold foreign exchange balances and carry out conversions into (and from) domestic currency for the state foreign trade organizations. Since the price of domestic goods bears no necessary connection with world prices, or even with those of communist neighbors, exports may involve losses as well as profits. The Foreign Trade Banks retain and channel into the budget any surplus of export proceeds over the amount to which the producers would normally be entitled according to the domestic value of their products and, conversely, they distribute to the producers any subsidies that may be required when export prices are set lower than domestic costs.

To encourage the sale of exports for convertible currencies, several countries (notably Hungary and Czechoslovakia) have in recent years paid exporting enterprises a bonus in such currencies, according to complex scales in which the rate of retention of foreign exchange rises sharply with the percentage by which exports exceed planned volume. Under a new system introduced in Czechoslovakia in 1966, an enterprise's share in foreign exchange earnings not only increases progressively with plan overfulfillment, but also is differentiated in accordance with the goods sold, their destination, and the kind of foreign exchange involved.

96

The producer will be able to utilize such foreign exchange earnings for improving productivity (by purchasing foreign equipment, licenses, patents, and so on) and for meeting travel expenses of engineers, sales representatives, and other personnel. A similar program was introduced in East Germany as early as 1954. The attractiveness of such schemes is further enhanced when the foreign exchange so earned can be utilized, within prescribed limits, at the discretion of the individual enterprise and with a minimum of bureaucratic interference.

Although the communist countries have been making great efforts to obtain foreign credits to finance imports, in particular of capital goods and agricultural products, they must always finance their own exports, since they do not have access to third-country financing. Thus enterprises that produce exclusively or predominantly for export normally receive bank credit not only for their production costs—which may include the cost of imported raw materials—but also to bridge the period before receipt of the proceeds for the goods sold abroad. Because exports are of particularly crucial importance to the smaller communist countries, the principles of socialist credit are occasionally set aside to permit interunit credit if it will stimulate export production. For example, since 1957, Hungarian foreign trade organizations have had the authority, under certain conditions, to provide domestic enterprises with credit for purchasing abroad equipment that would expand their output of exportable goods. In general, foreign trade activities compel communist countries to use financing techniques and instruments that are common in noncommunist countries and, in dealing with enterprises producing for export, to show greater flexibility and offer greater incentives than in the case of enterprises producing for the domestic market exclusively.

CONTROL OF FOREIGN PAYMENTS

Nothing is known about the size or management of the gold or foreign exchange reserves of the Eastern European countries. The size of the Soviet Union's gold production is a matter of guesswork (Rumania is the only other gold producer in the area). Basically, each country of Eastern Europe manages its foreign exchange reserves independently, occasionally obtaining foreign exchange or even gold loans from the stronger partners, mainly the Soviet Union.

The State Bank exercises complete control over all foreign exchange transactions, and it alone (and, under its control, the Foreign Trade and Foreign Exchange Banks, where these exist) can deal in foreign exchange. Management of foreign exchange holdings—from the establishment of foreign exchange budgets to decisions on the distribution of exchange balances among various currencies and depositories—involves close cooperation between the State Bank and the Ministry of Finance, in which the final authority apparently resides in most cases. Each State Bank establishes a single official exchange rate for each foreign currency; this rate is based on gold parities and is applied uniformly to all commercial transactions.

The exchange rate for noncommercial payments between the communist countries is computed by applying fixed "coefficients" to the official parity rates. These coefficients, which are supposed to adjust official rates to differences in the actual cost of living, may result in rates for noncommercial payments that are above or below the parities based on the gold content of the pairs of currencies involved. As Table 6 shows, the disparities may be quite substantial. Thus the Polish zloty equivalent of the Russian ruble for noncommercial payments is less

TABLE 6

FOREIGN EXCHANGE RATES OF EASTERN EUROPEAN CURRENCIES FOR "COMMERCIAL" AND "NONCOMMERCIAL" TRANSACTIONS

Country	Monetary unit	Gold content per monetary unit (in grams)	USSR rubles per 100 monetary units		United States dollars per 100 monetary units	
			Commercial rate	Noncommercial rate	Commercial rate	Noncommercial rate
Bulgaria .... Lev		0.759548	76.92	128.21	85.47	50.00
Czechoslovakia .. Koruna		0.123426	12.50	10.36	13.89	6.17
East Germany ... Mark		0.399902	40.50	31.25	45.05	23.81
Hungary .... Forint		0.075758	7.67	7.63	8.52	4.26
Poland .... Zloty		0.222168	22.50	6.54	25.00	4.17
Rumania .... Leu		0.148112	15.00	12.05	16.67	8.33 / 5.56*
USSR .... Ruble		0.987412	—	—	111.11	111.11

*Tourist rate.

Sources: *L. I. Frei*, Mezhdunarodnye raschety i finansirovanie vneshnei torgovli sotsialisticheskikh stran *(International Settlements and Financing of Foreign Trade of Socialist Countries), Moscow, 1965, pages 46, 126, 201;* SBZ von A bis Z *(Bonn), 1965, page 467; First National City Bank, New York.*

than one third of the official parity; on the other hand, the Bulgarian lev commands more than a 50 per cent premium in noncommercial transactions with the Soviet Union. Additional special conversion rates are used in certain cases. Perhaps the most important of these are the coefficients used in determining each country's actual contribution to various jointly undertaken investment projects: various categories of imports (such as individual building materials, machinery, labor) are converted by means of complex computations designed to correct for disparities in domestic price levels.[1] This is merely one instance of the expedients made necessary by a price system based, not on relative scarcities and factor costs, but on administrative decisions embodying a variety of not necessarily consistent considerations, which differ also from country to country.

With the exception of the Soviet Union (since its currency reform of 1961), all the communist countries exchange tourist funds and other noncommercial payments from noncommunist countries at a favorable exchange rate, by paying a fixed premium in addition to the official rate. Foreigners must exchange their remaining local currency before leaving any Eastern European country; at least in the Soviet Union, a check denominated in sterling is issued if the convertible currency originally exchanged is not available at the point of exit.

A communist country's annual plans for international payments (foreign exchange budgets) are prepared for each nation with which it trades. Such plans are aggregated by currency area, and are ultimately incorporated in an overall plan, with three main subdivisions of payments: those in convertible currencies, those cleared through the IBEC, and those cleared through bilateral accounts. Obviously, its planning of payments with capitalist countries must take into consideration not only its own import needs and export capabilities (and related plans) but also price fluctuations and the cyclical and other influences relevant to its ability to buy and sell in those markets.[2] The trade conducted on the basis of bilateral clearing agreements tends to present considerable difficulty in many instances, and entails ingenious schemes for the disposal of unwanted balances. At times these schemes involve third countries with convertible currencies. In

---

[1] *See the article by K. Larionov and N. Obolensky, "Fruitful Cooperation in the Realm of Foreign Exchange and Financial Relations", Finansy SSSR, January 1965.*

[2] *The communist countries' growing volume of foreign credits—those obtained from the West and those extended to or obtained from other communist countries—have made it necessary for them to establish special plans showing foreign indebtedness by currency and maturity.*

1965, for instance, Czechoslovakia transferred its credit balances with Guinea to the United Kingdom as partial payment for a ship purchased from the United Kingdom; the latter then used the funds to purchase ore in Guinea.

INTERNATIONAL PAYMENTS MECHANISM

In the Soviet Union the institutional arrangements for international payments and other foreign exchange activities and for the financing of foreign trade underwent a number of changes during the period between the two World Wars. After World War II the other countries of Eastern Europe, which had had quite active international banking contacts with Western Europe, were anxious to rebuild their prewar trade and banking relations with the Western world. The arrangements they have developed represent a mixture of elements borrowed from the Soviet Union and survivals from earlier mechanisms (such as the Foreign Exchange Board in Hungary).

With the exception of Rumania, all Eastern European countries have found it convenient to establish separate Foreign Trade Banks. These are organized along the lines of commercial banks in Western countries (although their capital is typically held by a number of official institutions, such as the Ministries of Finance and of Foreign Trade and the State Bank), and great effort is made to create the impression abroad that they operate exactly as any private commercial bank abroad. The Foreign Trade Bank is in charge of all payments related to foreign trade and international service transactions; in addition it provides credit to export and import organizations and in most cases also to certain enterprises that specialize in manufacturing export goods. Each country's Foreign Trade Bank participates in the multilateral clearing arrangements of the IBEC.

Typically the Foreign Trade Bank consists of a single office in the capital city (in Czechoslovakia, with its highly specialized export industries, two branches are maintained in the centers of such industries), using elsewhere local offices of the State Bank as agents. The relationship of the Foreign Trade Bank to the State Bank is very close; indeed, the former has usually evolved from the Foreign Department of the latter. In several instances the process of separation entailed transferring most accounts with foreign commercial banks to the newly formed Foreign Trade Bank. The State Bank thus retained, in addition to its central bank connections, only a limited number of foreign commercial bank accounts. As a rule the head of the Foreign Trade Bank serves as a member of the Board of Managers of the State Bank, and there is also some interchange of personnel.

100

The volume of exchange and the prices stipulated in trade agreements with Western countries, and with most underdeveloped countries, are expressed in Western currencies. The obtaining of foreign trade credit abroad, including vendor credits for the acquisition of capital goods, has become a main consideration of official policies in all Eastern European countries. Their State and Foreign Trade Banks have become actively engaged in negotiating credit lines with foreign commercial banks, frequently endeavoring to reestablish traditional banking relationships (such as those between Hungary and Austria). They have also established extensive correspondent relationships with banks in the West and throughout the world.

In each country, as has been mentioned, the management of international payments is organized in three patterns. Payments within the bloc are now uniformly channeled through the IBEC, with the State Bank typically in charge of preparing the annual payments plans and the related credit plans, and the Foreign Trade Bank in charge of the day-to-day operating contacts with the IBEC. For intrabloc payments the problem consists of drawing up an annual plan that will balance. In contrast, financial relations with the West require careful budgeting of exchange earnings and negotiations of needed credits, and thus a separate foreign exchange budget is prepared for countries with convertible currencies. The reestablishment of trade relations with noncommunist countries originally involved the same rigorous balancing of payments between trade partners that still characterizes trade among communist countries, but now bilateral payments involving convertible-currency countries are no longer necessarily balanced every year, although there is a clear tendency to balance trade exchanges. This trade is usually based on long-term agreements, frequently supplemented by annual "protocols". The third category of international payments flows involves countries with nonconvertible currencies, with which trade is based on bilateral agreements; most underdeveloped countries belong in this category. All such payments are cleared through accounts maintained by the respective central (or State) banks. Any foreign aid that involves cash payments or the extension of credits to underdeveloped nations by the Eastern European countries is channeled through the official banks, which receive budgetary appropriations and foreign exchange funds earmarked for such purposes.

The job of capturing the maximum foreign exchange from foreign tourists and other travelers, like that serving the needs of embassies and of citizens entitled to an allocation of foreign exchange for trips abroad, is left in the hands of the State Bank. In some countries, notably Hungary, the Foreign Trade Bank engages in currency exchange and other service activities, but ordinarily these are performed by the State Bank, which usually maintains special facilities at hotels, tourist resorts, and international conventions for facilitating the exchange of foreign currency and traveler's checks.

TRAVEL FUNDS AND REMITTANCES

Citizens of the countries of Eastern Europe can receive foreign exchange either through remittances or as payment for services (such as royalties), but in most countries they must convert it into the national currency or spend it in special stores. In Poland and Czechoslovakia, the Foreign Exchange Banks make it possible for local residents to maintain foreign exchange accounts that originate in remittances (in convertible currency); such accounts can be drawn on to buy local or imported goods at advantageous prices at special stores, and can also be converted into local currency or used abroad. Where such specialized banks do not exist, either the State Bank or the Foreign Trade Bank provides limited and strictly regulated opportunities for nationals and foreigners to maintain accounts in foreign currencies, which can be used abroad or converted into local currency. In most of the countries foreigners may open two kinds of such accounts: one (called "Account B" in the Soviet Union) can be used only for making domestic payment (after conversion into the local currency); the other ("Account A") can be used also for making payments or retransferring funds abroad.

With the considerable growth of travel among the countries of Eastern Europe, as well as greater contact with other countries, the original very stringent rules for currency exchange have been relaxed somewhat, and the limited facilities provided for it have been expanded. But the strict prohibition of the export or import of currency still applies. The primary and avowed aim of this prohibition is to prevent the development of free markets—and considerable discount from parity values—for notes of the Eastern European countries.[3] Thus the Gosbank will automatically buy notes or checks on banks of a noncommunist country

---

[3] *Since 1963, Soviet citizens have been permitted to take out of the country a limited amount of rubles—equivalent to $33—which, however, they must have with them when reentering the USSR; this permits returning travelers to make small travel expenditures upon reentering the USSR without wasting time at exchange booths at the point of entry. Similar regulations exist in the other Eastern European communist countries.*

(although those in nonconvertible currencies are accepted only "on consignment"), but it will not freely exchange the bank notes of any communist country.

Funds for travel in communist countries are usually carried in traveler's checks denominated in the currency of the country the tourist plans to visit; these checks, introduced in 1955, are issued by each State Bank for sale by all the other State Banks. For example, Soviet tourists to Rumania would pay rubles to the State Bank of the Soviet Union for the purchase of traveler's checks issued in lei by the State Bank of Rumania. Since 1958 the State Bank of the Soviet Union has issued checks denominated in sterling, mostly for travelers to noncommunist countries; these are now cashable in more than sixty nations and are also issued by its correspondents in some countries.

THE INTERNATIONAL BANK FOR ECONOMIC COOPERATION

The settlement of payments among the countries of Eastern Europe was multilateralized at the start of 1964, when the IBEC began operating in Moscow (the agreement establishing it was signed October 22, 1963).[4] All Eastern European countries (not including Yugoslavia and Albania) are members of the bank, as is also Outer Mongolia. The establishment of the bank followed several years of not very successful experimentation with triangular clearing (for limited categories of transactions), under the sponsorship of the Council for Mutual Economic Assistance (COMECON). The latter was organized in 1949 as a counterweight to the Organization for European Economic Cooperation, and had quite ambitious objectives for coordinating the economies of its members.

The IBEC's authorized capital is 300 million rubles ($330 million at the official exchange rate), to be paid by the members in transferable rubles, convertible exchange, or gold in five annual instalments. Each country's share has been set in accordance with a formula based on its participation in intrabloc trade; the shares range from 38.7 per cent for the Soviet Union to 1 per cent for Outer Mongolia. The internal organization of the IBEC bears some resemblance to that of the Bretton Woods institutions. Its governing bodies are a Bank Council—which meets quarterly (in various member countries) and by

---

[4] *Even before the bank's creation practically all payments among its members were made by mutual offsets (95 per cent for the Soviet Union in 1960). The bank's activities may, however, have contributed to some growth of trade among its members.*

103

unanimous vote determines general policy, including credit and other operating plans—and a Managing Board in charge of day-to-day operations.[5]

During the first two years of its existence, the IBEC's operations were almost exclusively limited to the multilateral clearing of payments of the eight participating countries, very much along the lines of the old European Payments Union. The main purpose of shifting to multilateral clearings was to increase the volume of intrabloc trade and to achieve a more rational use of the resources and export capabilities of the participating countries. Subsidiary considerations involved possible substitution of intrabloc trade for imports from the West and reduction of the required export financing. But the agreement that established the IBEC envisaged a wider scope of activities than multilateral clearing, the details to be worked out in future negotiations and decisions by the bank's governing body. These broader goals include bank financing of joint investment projects by two or more of its members and the provisions of deposit and investment facilities for convertible and other currencies deposited with the bank at the discretion of member countries. This foreign exchange, as well as gold received on deposit, could be either loaned to members or invested in the Western money markets. So far, little if anything has been done in either direction. Such joint projects as are undertaken continue to be financed directly by the participating countries, and all member countries still prefer to employ directly whatever foreign exchange balances they may have available. Nor has anything been done to implement the original intentions of channeling through the bank the individual members' aid to underdeveloped countries. An invitation to other countries to participate in the bank's clearing arrangements has so far remained unheeded, even by Cuba and Yugoslavia.

The clearing operations of the bank are conducted in "transferable rubles". Although this unit is defined in terms of gold (0.987412 grams) and is equivalent to the ruble of the Soviet Union, it is not freely convertible either into that currency or into any other monetary unit. It is thus nothing more than a conventional internal accounting unit, in which all claims and payments in national currencies are stated on the basis of fixed exchange rates, and in which the bank's loans to the participating countries and the members' credit or debit balances are denominated.

---

[5] The "Agreement on Multilateral Settlements in Transferable Rubles and the Organization of the International Bank for Economic Cooperation" and the "Statutes of the International Bank for Economic Cooperation" appeared in Vneshniaia Torgovlia, August 1964, pages 47-55.

Clearings are based on annual payments plans submitted to the bank by each member. In these plans, payments by each country to all partners combined—not only trade payments but also invisibles and credits extended among the participating countries—must balance against projected total receipts from the same group of countries. Thus the clearing arrangements, though they provide for the financing of seasonal and other temporary deficits through the bank, embody the basic principle of maintaining continuous balance in the intrabloc accounts of each communist country (balancing payments between pairs of countries is not required). In practice, such balancing within the COMECON group is possible only because in many cases the prices stipulated in the bilateral agreements that underlie the members' trade relations bear no relationship either to domestic prices and costs or to the cost of comparable goods that can be purchased or sold for convertible currency. During the first year of operations (1964), virtually all payments arising from intrabloc trade (amounting to almost $25 billion) were cleared through the IBEC. Noncommercial payments, originally cleared through a separate account, were later pooled with trade payments.

The need to resort to bank financing arises whenever a member's imports (and other payments) run ahead of its receipts.[6] In the first year, only 10 per cent of the trade payments cleared required bank financing (for an average of twenty-five days), a substantial reduction from the volume of bilateral trade credit required under the old system. The total volume of credit outstanding fluctuated between 300 million and 350 million rubles during the summer and fall months of 1964, and was much lower during the remainder of the year. More than two thirds of the credit extended was for bridging payments gaps; on such credit, a "swing line" (in 1964, 2½ per cent of the planned trade volume) is available interest free, but 2 per cent is charged on the remaining funds. Other credits, at 1½ per cent, are granted for normal seasonal needs, and also—for a duration of up to two years—to finance imports above the volume stipulated in trade agreements. Repayments of this latter type of credit, intended to stimulate expansion of intra-COMECON trade, must be included in the members' clearing plans for the following year.

[6] *The IBEC uses the "subsequent acceptance" payments method, which provides for immediate debiting of the payer's account, giving him the right to have the entry reversed for valid reasons. Each day, by telex, the bank receives from each participant a payments claim in which collections for its various exporting organizations are consolidated by country; debits are then made to the account of the importing countries.*

The IBEC's operations were initiated before agreement could be reached on many aspects of its future activities. Discussion on these is continuing, but according to the limited amount of information that has become available, even the operation of a multilateral clearing system has raised serious questions as to the future of the bank and has brought into the open considerable conflicts of views and interests. Indeed, the most important immediate problems are directly tied to multilateral clearing. Each participating country desires to increase its purchases from the West, even though, under present arrangements, any expansion of trade must balance within the bloc after allowing for any balance for noncommercial payments. Thus the nonconvertibility of transferable rubles creates a dilemma whenever there is a possibility to increase (absolutely or relatively) exports outside the COMECON and thereby earn convertible currency rather than accepting the less desirable goods (in terms of kind, quality, or price) that the other members can offer in exchange. As a result, the shift to multilateral clearings through the IBEC—while it has shortened collection delays, reduced the need for trade credit, and facilitated expansion of intrabloc trade—has also increased pressures for more realistic pricing of goods traded and for convertibility of balances. Since convertibility would require payment in gold or convertible currencies by those countries that are unable to balance their intrabloc payments, even the introduction of partial convertibility (up to a given percentage of surpluses) would present difficult problems. These have been discussed by the participating countries ever since the bank was launched.

Obviously, those countries that have a real option between exports to the East and to the West, such as Poland and Hungary, have the strongest desire to move on to at least partial convertibility (which, in practice, might mean obtaining gold or convertible exchange from the Soviet Union). Other countries, including Rumania which has relatively large foreign exchange earnings, are less dependent on convertibility of IBEC surpluses. At the bottom of the whole discussion about convertibility lies the question of greater flexibility in intrabloc relations, since no relaxation of the present requirement that each country balance its payments each year can be envisaged unless surpluses can be used outside the area. Such steps as have been taken so far—establishment of reciprocal accounts in convertible currencies by pairs of participating countries, or collection in convertible exchange of part of the capital subscriptions payable in 1966—are of limited scope and serve merely to underline the basic problem arising from multilateral clearings conducted in a nonconvertible currency.

There is considerable evidence in fact that deliveries fell behind agreed levels, that in some cases considerable credit balances tended to accumulate in spite of efforts to find means to balance transactions, and that dissatisfaction with the way the IBEC has been developing is widespread.

SOVIET-OWNED BANKS IN FOREIGN COUNTRIES

Banks in Eastern Europe maintain correspondent relationships with commercial banks in the United States and in Western Europe. In addition, Soviet-owned banks in Western countries give the State and Foreign Trade Banks of communist countries (not only those covered in the present study) a point of contact with the money markets of the West for dealings in gold and convertible currencies and for participation in the Euro-dollar market. This section is devoted to Soviet-owned banks abroad, of which the two commercial banks now active in Western Europe are of particular importance. Their facilities are extensively used by the State and Foreign Trade Banks of the communist countries of Europe and Asia, and also by Cuba.

One of these, the Moscow Narodny Bank, was originally established in London during World War I as an agency of a Russian bank for cooperatives. The other, the Banque Commerciale pour l'Europe du Nord, was founded in Paris in 1921 by Russian anticommunist émigrés but was bought by Soviet interests four years later. The shares of both banks are owned entirely by various official entities of the Soviet Union. (A third bank owned by the authorities of the Soviet Union, Voskhod, was organized in 1966 in Zurich.)

These two banks have developed rapidly since the late 1950's in the wake of expanding East-West trade, the growing diversification of the trade of Eastern Europe, the growth of European money markets, and the success of the Soviet Union and the other countries in obtaining private and government guaranteed or insured credits from the West. Both banks are active in financing the foreign trade of Eastern Europe, in which they are eager to interest commercial banks of Western countries. To this end they act as collection and payments agents for official foreign trade and banking organizations, and otherwise endeavor to develop any type of business that would be normal for a commercial bank of a Western country specializing in foreign trade. They also serve as agents for gold sales by the Soviet Union, invest the temporarily free foreign exchange of all communist countries, and engage in various operations in convertible currency (including Euro-dollars) on behalf of the banks of the communist countries. The Narodny Bank, which in the twenties had branches in New York, Paris, and

Berlin, opened a branch in Beirut in 1963.[7] Although the Foreign Exchange Bank of Poland and that of Czechoslovakia have several branches abroad, they serve mostly to channel remittances from emigrants and to accommodate similar transactions that result in foreign exchange earnings, rather than to finance foreign trade.

8. New Policies and New Credit Techniques

All the centrally planned economies of Eastern Europe bear the hallmarks of their historical origin. Their Soviet prototype was originally created to cope with a situation of overall shortages inherited from years of war and civil war; whatever industry was able to produce found eager takers, as the output of consumer goods could not keep pace with the demand. But the system began to break down when excess demand for consumer goods ceased to be the dominant factor in the economy. As supplies increased, the consumers' refusal to buy what was inferior, unfashionable, or overpriced tended to load distribution channels with unsalable products. This occurred in the late 1950's, to a varying degree, in all the countries of Eastern Europe. The resulting accumulation of unwanted inventories caused disruptions in the planned turnover of working capital and hence an increase of overdue loans. Other shortcomings of the system became exposed, as foreign trade developed and as freer travel permitted wider comparisons of economic performance. Countries that before World War II had engaged in a relatively open system of foreign trade and travel became more sharply aware of the cost, in opportunities foregone, of adhering to the rigid Soviet patterns of trade bilateralism and internal economic centralization.

---

[7] *Between the two World Wars, foreign trade banks owned by official Soviet interests operated in several other countries of Europe and Asia. After World War II, the Soviet-owned Garantie- und Kreditbank was established in the Soviet sector of Berlin. It evolved from the prewar Garantie- und Kreditbank für den Osten, and its main activities, prior to its liquidation, centered around the payments that had arisen from the flow of postwar reparations and the maintenance of Soviet occupation troops. It also administered funds provided by the East German government for occupation costs and acted on behalf of Soviet foreign trade organizations in East Germany. The bank had several regional branches throughout that country.*

108

Many of the shortcomings of centrally planned economies are now widely recognized in Eastern Europe. Critical voices in these countries (where all audible voices have at least some degree of official approval) are raising questions about the ability of their economic system to achieve optimum utilization of resources and to identify and put into effect the most efficient methods of production.

It is not claimed by the authorities in Eastern Europe that failings of the monetary and credit system as such are by themselves responsible in any significant degree for the most glaring shortcomings. To be sure, monetary policy has in some cases contributed to inflationary developments; and the failure of the agriculture of most countries to assure adequate supplies may have been aggravated by the low priority given to farm credit, just as the nature of credit administration may have contributed to the interminable delays and poor quality in industrial construction, another area in which performance has been uniformly deficient. But although all major difficulties have monetary and credit aspects, it remains true that in the past credit had not been used either to guide economic activity or to achieve corrective action.

Some of the basic causes of these difficulties are unrealistic, inflexible, and excessively detailed planning, lack of initiative as a consequence of insufficient incentives, inadequate response to consumer preferences, faulty allocation of investment, and—perhaps above all—a price system that does not reflect all elements of cost and relies primarily on administrative controls to cope with disequilibria. A rational allocation of existing resources, and the development of additional resources, requires a substantially different pricing system. It is in this general context that the new credit techniques now being developed and to some degree applied in the various countries of Eastern Europe must be considered. Their measure of success will hinge on the nature of related changes in the non-financial sphere.

NATURE OF THE REFORMS

The economic reforms now being envisaged fall into two broad categories. In one group are those that aim at greater efficiency in pursuing the existing policies— by trying to dismantle excesses in centralization, to decentralize decision making, to give greater authority and scope to the managers of enterprises, to simplify procedures, to curb the power of bureaucrats, and to give greater weight to judgments of experts. Such changes are frequently referred to as improvement of the management (or "steering") of the economy. In a broader sense they represent the never-ending search for the "centralization-decentralization balance", which has been an important aspect of the various organizational changes in the Soviet economy over the last decade and which has had reverberations in the other countries of Eastern Europe. Reforms of the second type go further. They aim, in effect, at creating a socialist economic system that would rely to the greatest degree possible on impersonal "economic levers"—that is, competition, material incentives, and objective criteria, such as the rate of profits. These reforms would confine central planning to macroplanning, which would encompass only basic politico-economic decisions with regard to the distribution of the national product and the desirable rate of growth. They would also leave greater room for individual initiative and place less reliance on detailed bureaucratic directives and controls as a substitute for market responses to assessable alternatives. Planning periods would be lengthened, and the number of indicators included in plans would be reduced radically.

Taken together, these two types of reforms represent a move toward greater autonomy of individual enterprises and reduced administrative interference from the center. In fact, the COMECON countries, without conceding it and frequently denying it, now seem ready to follow in many respects—more timidly and, in most cases, with an exaggerated emphasis on continuity in their own policies— the example set more than a decade ago by Yugoslavia.

While the details and emphases of the new policies differ from country to country, they share certain essential principles. These have been summarized as follows by one of the originators and leading proponents:[1]

> The national plan should determine only the basic macroeconomic developments;
> In the interest of the independent operative decisions of enterprises, reliance on the compulsory centrally directed volume indicators must be given up;
> The enterprises must have substantial influence on the drafting of the central perspective plans, in particular on the choice of profitable new investment projects;
> Desirable development must be achieved by means of coordinated, but centrally determined, economic regulations and instruments (taxes, prices, structure of income and rewards, credit, interest, etc.);
> Enterprises must cover costs, particularly wages, from revenue only, not from subsidies;
> Prices must reflect costs and help to close the gap between supply and demand.

---

[1] *Ota Šik, "Socialist Commodity and Money Relations and the New System of Planned Management",* Politická Ekonomie, *April 1965.*

There are, of course, considerable differences among the individual countries. In some, where there is quite outspoken disenchantment with reliance on total and detailed planning and administrative enforcement of compliance, it is recognized that greater dependence of material incentives and managerial initiative will make it not only possible but necessary to give up the elaborate financial controls that have proved ineffective. But in the Soviet Union, there is still a tendency to make the new policies appear to be merely a logical development of existing policies; efforts are still directed primarily toward "improving" controls rather than diminishing them. The general shift to a system of material incentives and rewards, now under way, in combination with greater reliance on credit as a tool of indirect leverage, ought ultimately to lead to a gradual retreat from the State Bank's direct involvement in filling managerial voids and to a cutting through the administrative complexities that characterize Soviet-type economies.

Obviously, to the extent that significant moves from reliance on total planning and central command have been initiated, considerable changes will ensue in the area of banking and credit. But, as was stressed above, the true significance of these changes will be revealed only after it becomes clear how far and how fast the individual countries are willing to go in changing from command (centrally planned) to demand (market) economies. There is still a question to what degree the current trend toward greater reliance on economic levers, indirect inducements, and material stimulation will eventuate in a reduction of centralized planning in terms of physical quantities. There is considerable evidence of resistance to the new ideas, and of attempts to limit their implementation. This is true not only for the more radical changes, like those in Czechoslovakia, but even for the hesitant steps to which the Soviet Union has committed itself.

The reforms now being introduced involve significant changes in financial flows and in the role that credit is expected to play in the economy. They will increase the role of banks—without significantly changing their character—in channeling (gross) investment funds and in financing the flow of raw materials and intermediary and final products. As a result, it may be expected that the size of the national budget, in relation to the national product, will decline and the amount of decentralized investment funds and bank loans will increase.

The nature and the future of the reforms being introduced in the area of banking are closely related to the more basic changes that are under way. Two categories of such changes are of particular relevance, the first involving production and the second investment.

Factories (at least in the consumer goods area) will plan production on the basis of orders actually received, in most cases directly, from retail outlets or on the basis of negotiated contracts. They will have to adapt production to changes in consumer preferences, and the management's success will be judged by the rate of profit rather than by its ability to hit detailed output targets. Management will be given greater scope for making decisions. The relatively small part of profits previously retained by individual enterprises to provide bonus payments to management and to the entire staff (in cash or in the form of fringe benefits, such as housing, vacation trips, nurseries) will be increased, and its size geared to the achievement of planned or higher-than-planned profits.[2] Simultaneously, performance will be gauged by only a small number of indicators, among which the profit rate assumes the key role. Wherever possible, vertical integration or horizontal combination of related plants into large concerns (industry associations) will be encouraged, in order to permit, among other things, greater specialization of production and decentralization of planning, with much of the planning originating within the new affiliations of plants.[3] There is a tendency to lengthen the planning period and to avoid frequent changes in plans.

The other basic change that deserves special consideration is in the area of capital formation and cost accounting. Under the Soviet system, no charge was made for capital, on the theory that it was public property; the result was malallocation of investment, since a larger investment per unit of output was not necessarily reflected in higher costs. Now it is being recognized that producer prices must reflect the cost of capital. To improve its allocation, interest is to be charged on both fixed and working capital, although there are some differences in the application of this principle in the various countries; and to equalize the cost of new and existing capital, a charge is being imposed on the depreciated volume of fixed capital assets in use.[4] In effect, the charge for capital means that some of the amounts previously transferred to the budget as enterprise profits

---

[2] *In determining profits, however, it is not easy to get away from the bureaucratic procedures and artificialities inherent in a planned economy with centrally prescribed prices. In Poland, for instance, when it was decided to relate payments into the "enterprise fund" to improvements in profits, a special corps of government accounting experts was created to adjust profit statements of two successive years for influences "beyond the control" of the given enterprise, in order to determine the year-to-year change in the "true" profit margin.*

[3] *See R. Evstigneev, "Industrial Amalgamations in Some Socialist Countries"*, Voprosy Ekonomiki, September 1965.

[4] *There is still considerable tendency to find euphemisms for interest, such as "production fund contribution"* (Produktionsfondsabgabe) *in East Germany.*

are now paid by the enterprise under the heading of interest. Again, while the underlying principle now seems to have been accepted by all countries of Eastern Europe, its practical application is likely to be gradual and to vary from country to country. In Hungary, such a charge (at the uniform rate of 5 per cent) was introduced in 1964; the specific details are now being worked out in Poland; and introduction of the principle is still being studied in East Germany, Czechoslovakia, and the Soviet Union.[5] One major problem is that the introduction of a charge for capital will increase the number of enterprises operating at a loss. The new system will make a real difference only when investment decisions begin to be made on the basis of alternatives involving the cost of capital as one of the elements considered.

THE NEW ROLE OF CREDIT IN CAPITAL FORMATION

The role of credit in capital formation will increase, as the external financing of fixed capital is shifted from a grant to a loan basis and as a large part of investment comes to be financed from internal sources. With these developments, bank credit will be used not only to finance investment projects (to be amortized from future profits and depreciation reserves) but also to bridge temporary gaps and deficiencies in the flow of internal funds earmarked for investment and development purposes.

The following discussion of the new system of investment financing in Poland may serve to bring out the main features that are being, or have been, introduced in one form or another in the individual countries of Eastern Europe. There will be three methods of financing fixed investment in industry: budgetary grants, "own" resources, and bank loans. Certain projects of national importance (such as defense factories or the introduction of new industries or processes), designated in Poland as "priority projects", will continue to be financed from budgetary resources, though funds to meet expenses in excess of planned costs have to be loan financed and amortized out of future profits. Other centrally planned investment projects will be financed by loans, which will be retired from future profits and depreciation allowances. Lending terms, including interest rates, will be used

---

[5] *For the effective operation of the new system, it is apparently considered essential that the interest rate charged for long-term investment be uniform and that any social and national priorities be implemented by overt subsidies.*

to achieve completion of construction and installation of machinery within contractual dates and cost estimates; penalty rates are to be charged for credit needs arising from delays, with such interest costs charged against an enterprise's reserve funds—another means of substituting pecuniary motives for administrative supervision.[6]

For the first time, internally generated funds will become a significant direct source of financing. Two funds are to be constituted for this purpose: one through the retention of a stipulated part of profits and depreciation allowances by individual enterprises, and the other through channeling of a part of these resources into investment funds of industry associations. These industrywide or regional aggregations of enterprises will have considerable latitude in selecting investment projects and determining financing procedures. Individual enterprises may use their own "investment funds" for implementing projects approved by the planning authorities, and also they will be free to undertake projects on their own responsibility, provided they can obtain bank financing for the purpose. The national credit plan will include a reserve, equivalent to 10 per cent of the cost of planned investments of enterprises, for extending credit to finance projects not included in the investment plan. A further step would be the transfer of all investment funds from the budget to a special "fund for economic development" which would permit planning of investment financing (through credit, grants, subsidies, or whatever) on a longer than annual basis. Proposals to this effect are under study at least in Czechoslovakia, where reforms very similar to those of Poland are currently being introduced. It is now recognized that greater reliance on credit in the framework of such an overall policy would permit a more effective allocation of scarce resources.[7]

The ultimate objective of the new arrangements is to achieve a more rational pattern of investment in productive capital and a reduction of the investment-output ratio. Financing from internally generated funds or through repayable loans (as contrasted with nonrepayable grants)—guided by the profit expectations of alternative projects—is expected to reduce the waste in real resources (a now widely criticized by-product of grant financing), to speed up the com-

---

[6] D. Butakov, "Innovations in Financing of Industry in Poland", Finansy SSSR, November 1965.

[7] See Karel Suchan, "Financial Relations in the Economic System of Management", Politická Ekonomie, April 1965, and John M. Montias, "Economic Reform in Perspective", Survey, April 1966.

pletion of new projects, and to provide a logical way for introducing the cost of capital as one of the factors of production. Loan financing of investment is being used as an indirect tool ("lever") to achieve results that central command and detailed control could not deliver.

It is readily evident that the new system of investment financing (including the introduction of a charge on existing capital) will have important implications for the price system, for the allocation of real resources, for financial flows, and for the operation of the entire economic system. The portion of investment funds channeled through the national budget will be reduced considerably (making the budget more similar to those of capitalist countries). Only part of these funds will continue to finance investment on a nonreturnable grant basis, as the bulk will augment the revolving fund of the Investment Bank. On the other hand, individual enterprises, as has been emphasized, will have a larger amount of "own" funds for financing their investment (in some countries, even the right to use capital repair and maintenance funds for the acquisition of new equipment), and will also be able to choose among alternative projects in making financing decisions.

Obviously, the role of the banking system will be substantially increased if bank credit financing of investment is substituted for budgetary grants in significant segments of the economy. Apart from that portion of investment funds which, though much reduced, will continue to be supplied on a grant basis, outside investment funds will no longer be a free good allocated by central planners. Individual enterprises will have to justify the profitability of projects for which they require financing. The State Bank or the Investment Bank will have considerable latitude in dealing with loan applications, so long as it does not exceed the overall ceiling on centrally accumulated funds available for this purpose. This will be true both for long- and medium-term investment lending to state-owned enterprises and for lending to farm cooperatives for fixed capital purposes.

The shifting of a large part of plant and equipment financing from a grant to a loan basis will make the Investment Bank the manager of a growing revolving fund, continuously augmented by budgetary appropriations and by its own retained earnings. Investment Banks, instead of being predominantly disbursing agencies, will become involved in project appraisal and concerned with the prospective profitability of the projects to be financed, with lending terms (including maturity and rates), and with cash flow projections of enterprises.

The increased role assigned to industry associations as a source of investment as well as of short-term funds can be expected to result in considerable gains in flexibility and efficiency. These associations will assume a good deal of financial supervision over individual enterprises. In East Germany, they will be in charge of preparing cash flow plans (rather similar to those used by our corporations) that will identify the sources and uses of the funds at their disposal (as well as the flows into and from the budget).

CHANGES IN SHORT-TERM CREDITING

The primary aim of the new approach to investment financing is a better husbanding and allocation of investment funds, but short-term credit also presents opportunities for experimentation with a steering of the economy by incentives, rather than by administrative decisions. Some of the measures now being adopted are merely a continuation of the movement away from the multiplication of separate "objects of crediting", which began in the midfifties and has usually entailed giving greater latitude to the managers of the local offices of the State Bank. Its logical conclusion is a shift from making loans available for specific purposes only and secured by identifiable collateral to crediting on the basis of total sales ("turnover" in Soviet terminology).

Under this system, it is first determined, usually by superior economic organs, what part of the total working capital of each individual enterprise should consist of "own" funds, and what part should be borrowed; credit is then made available on an overall basis, without requiring detailed justification of the purpose of each advance, and the actual use of credit is left in the hands of the management, provided the unit is showing an adequate profit. For enterprises in other-than-seasonal industries, greater emphasis will be placed on making credit automatically available to finance a fixed (but not uniform) proportion of all expenditures for materials and wages. Thus, the amount of bank credit will fluctuate and grow with the volume of output without the need for new negotiations and paperwork. The proportions of the two components in the total remain constant, but the volume of credit changes over time with changes in overall capital needs, and it also fluctuates seasonally. In fact, when internal resources are not available to maintain the stipulated proportion of enterprise funds, the missing amount may be temporarily borrowed, either from the reserve fund of the industry association or from the State Bank (in the latter case, at a cost higher than that charged for the proportionate-share amount). It is clear that the shift toward making credit available on an overall basis requires substantial changes from past bank proce-

116

dures. The shift also makes it necessary—since reliance on mechanical procedures instead of informed judgment still prevails—for the enterprise itself to systematically separate its accounts and transactions pertaining to working capital from those pertaining to fixed assets, though this objective may not always be achieved.[8]

In several countries, industry associations or similar groupings will establish, in addition to the investment fund, separate funds for technological development, a reserve fund, and in some cases other special funds. The development and reserve funds will become, in effect, revolving funds from which temporary financial assistance will be available to member enterprises in the form of working- and fixed-capital loans for operating or development purposes.[9] They will become a source of credit to member enterprises when the bank refuses further loans because of failure to meet obligations stipulated in the credit agreement. The reserve fund will also provide guarantees for bank loans obtained by members that are experiencing financing difficulties.

The establishment of these association funds is tantamount to the creation of financial institutions for the servicing of specific industries, and thus introduces an entirely new element into the financial structure of communist countries. Obviously, credit needs differ greatly among industries and in accordance with the specific conditions of each enterprise. The new method of crediting will require a more intimate and current knowledge of the technology, the supply and demand conditions, and the profitability of each unit than under the old system. Since the late 1950's some attempts have been made to solve this problem by making one specific State Bank office responsible for the credit planning of large enterprises or of combines consisting of several units, but a further step has now been taken by the countries that have made provision for these industrywide reserve funds of associations—first Rumania, and later Czechoslovakia, Poland, and Hungary.

---

[8] *In Poland, for instance, resources from enterprises' "development funds" have been used in recent years to such an extent to finance minor investment projects that they became inadequate to fulfill their other purpose—to bring working capital up to required levels. In the future, resources will be accumulated during the entire year in an "Account A", to be transferred at the year-end to a disbursement "Account B", from which additional working-capital requirements will be covered before any fixed-capital expenditures are permitted.*

[9] *In East Germany, even loans to make tax and other payments to the government will be available from such sources. On the other hand, in Bulgaria and perhaps elsewhere, associations that include many low-profit units will receive budgetary grants to bolster their funds.*

117

East Germany, again taking a more radical step than its neighbors, has created within the framework of its monobank specialized divisions for the main branches of industry, with each such division ("Industrie-Bankfiliale", also called "Industriebank") servicing the credit needs of up to three associations. This reform (discussed more fully in Chapter 12) has enabled the monobank to combine the new industrial with the old territorial principle. The managers of the industrial divisions within the monobank are given the authority to set interest rate charges and to prescribe the form of settlements and the nature of credit sanctions, should these be required. Similar arrangements were introduced in mid-1965 in Czechoslovakia to conform with changes in the organization of industry. Special bank units will service the individual associations and be responsible for the bank's functions pertaining to the particular branch of industry. As in East Germany, these units will have close ties with their respective industry associations in regard to planning and implementation of economic policies and also oversee the activities of local bank branches in their relations with individual enterprises within the same association. This decentralization of lending is designed to increase the role of credit in guiding economic activity.

THE SIGNIFICANCE OF THE NEW POLICIES

Although the need for economic changes has been under discussion for several years, the countries of Eastern Europe have differed in their willingness—or ability—to identify the causes of the difficulties besetting their economies and to embark on sweeping changes. Thus progress in the direction of what can broadly be called a socialist market economy has been uneven. The most daring thinking and implementation, unexpectedly enough, are found in East Germany and Czechoslovakia, two countries in which the Stalinist intellectual heritage has lingered on longer than elsewhere; however, their economic performance has been particularly poor, especially in the years preceding the reforms. The Soviet Union, on the other hand, is exceedingly cautious in formulating a comprehensive new economic policy, although in the fall of 1965 it began to put into effect some reforms along the lines of those introduced by neighbors that have explicitly indicated their intention to move toward a socialist market economy. It is currently experimenting cautiously with alternative methods applied to selected enterprises and, in some cases, making related experiments in the areas of plant management, labor compensation, and the like. The Soviet Union commands a broader range of resources than its neighbors and for a variety of reasons

118

is not subject to the same pressures for change. And it has learned from bitter experience that mistakes made by a big, centralized country are usually also big and costly. Rumania's success with its current policies, which in some respects have been more flexible than those of the other planned economies, has tended to diminish its need to seek change. Poland and Hungary occupy an intermediary position. Bulgaria, which usually hews closely to Soviet attitudes, was the last country to announce reforms, but it is now apparently willing to try for a maximum of decentralization and flexibility. In some countries it is not denied that changes under way add up, in effect, to a recognition that market adjustments must become a basic process of economic growth. Other countries—including the Soviet Union—maintain that the new measures represent nothing more than a striving for better "steering of the economy" and that profit has always been an important criterion in Soviet-type systems. But recent experiences in Eastern Europe indicate that slow movers may overnight become daring innovators, while pioneers may turn timid.

Taken together, the new credit policies, although they may still pay lip service to the five principles of socialist credit, represent a radical departure from the standard system described in the preceding chapters. Up to now, the use of credit could not be envisaged from the point of view of its profitability, and availability of credit depended on administrative decisions. Although the efficient ("well-working") enterprises could expect particularly favorable treatment, this consisted in reduced red tape and lenience in applying excessively restrictive rules, rather than in lower rates. It is now intended to differentiate interest rates according to the purpose and character of borrowing; for instance, borrowing made necessary as a result of poor performance will be more costly. The need to husband borrowed funds—disregard of which has been a frequently criticized aspect of the prevailing system—will now be driven home by charging interest against the portion of profits available for bonus payments and other uses for the benefit of the staff. The credit rules and regulations may not diminish in number and complexity, but they will no longer be applied automatically. Credit relations will be based on agreements between the bank and the enterprise, rather than on the interpretation of applicable rules. It is thus only logical that the question is being raised, at least in some communist countries,[10] whether financial

---

[10] *For instance, in Poland; see D. Butakov, op. cit. (see footnote 6).*

performance (payment of bills and taxes when due, repayment of loans on maturity, and so on) should not be included among the criteria for judging the achievements of a given enterprise.

Behind the various organizational and procedural changes in the financing of fixed as well as working capital is a growing recognition in Eastern Europe of the fact that some economic principles, long regarded as applicable only to the capitalist system, are equally valid in the socialist economy. The allocative function of the market, the rationing function of prices, and the need for limitations on the power of the authorities to perpetuate disequilibrium situations are now widely recognized. Thus some communist countries are pursuing plans for revising the (still administratively determined) price structure to reflect more closely relative scarcities, comparative costs, and foreign prices.[11] As regards the credit system, the recognition of the role of interest as an equilibrium price and as a tool of economic policy is of particular importance.

In this area, Czechoslovakia has been perhaps more ready than its neighbors to cast the traditional communist views overboard. A few direct quotations from a pamphlet published in an official series designed to explain the new economic policy adopted at the end of 1965 may help to gauge the extent of the change. Observing that under conditions of relatively easy access to bank credit effective demand of producers tends to outrun available supplies, the official commentator remarks that "to slow down their demand by means of official resolutions and moral suasion is of no avail". It is possible, however, "to influence credit directly, and production and economic growth indirectly, by adjusting interest rates and credit terms". The logical conclusion is that the objective of credit policy is "to maintain balance between the volume of credit and the aims and possibilities of the economy". The writer of the pamphlet recognizes that equilibrium between the volume of loanable funds and aggregate demand for them must be established by varying interest rates, that some loan demand must go unsatisfied if monetary equilibrium is to be preserved, and that profitability should be the criterion for selecting among applicants when granting credit for either investment or working-

---

[11] *A leading East German economist, after reviewing approvingly the recent changes in investment financing, remarked "it is quite obvious that these measures are insufficient. It is necessary to resolve the question of whether the price mechanism could be used to achieve a further development of material stimuli": Otto Reinhold, "The New System of Planning and Management of the National Economy", Mirovaia Ekonomika i Mezhdunarodnye Otnosheniia, January 1966, page 104.*

capital purposes.[12] All this sounds familiar. But it is a far cry from the role assigned to money and credit in an economy that was expected to need money only as a common denominator and credit merely to bridge payment gaps, moving along on an equilibrium path staked out by all-knowing, all-powerful planners pushing levers that command material flows.

Decisions embodying the new philosophy have now been taken in all the countries covered by this study, except Rumania. Obviously, their implementation will take years, as specific procedures are still to be worked out and tested. Clearly, credit policy is not to supplant planning, but is rather to permit a reduction of its scope and to increase its effectiveness and flexibility. The total volume of credit available and the broad categories of its use will continue to be planned, in order to preserve monetary equilibrium. In the framework of the new policies, credit is to be regarded as a tauter string rather than as a looser leash. It will be used in conjunction with a different set of objectives and criteria. The effectiveness of the new use of credit will depend on the success in actually shifting a considerable part of decision making from central planners to enterprise managers.

These prospects are relevant to the question whether something identifiable as a "socialist monetary policy" is about to emerge. Even though an answer cannot yet be hazarded, it appears that the new developments are more likely to enhance the role of the monobank as a financial intermediary than to endow it with more attributes of a central bank in the Western sense. They will make the individual enterprise's access to credit increasingly dependent on its profitability, its financial position, and—indirectly at least—the quality of its management. But credit availability to the economy as a whole will continue to be centrally determined as a function of a national plan. Even significant steps toward some blend of centrally planned and market-oriented economies will not necessarily entail a basic change in the role of the banking system. The monobanker, permitted considerably more flexibility in dealing with microeconomic problems, will have an opportunity to become a more efficient commercial and investment banker, but there is no indication that he will be given wider responsibilities as a central banker.

---

[12] *M. Koudelka*, Finance a Úvěr v Nové Soustavé Rizeni *(Finances and Credit in the New System of Economic Administration), Prague, 1965.*

PART II

9. Soviet Union

The monetary and credit system of the Soviet Union was rebuilt from scratch after the victory of the Bolshevik revolution. One of the first acts of the new government was to nationalize all domestic and foreign banking institutions—their head offices in the capital having been taken over by armed detachments on a single day, December 14, 1917. Subsequently the monetary system underwent a series of radical changes: these included attempts during 1918-21 to abolish money; the introduction in 1924 of a uniform and stable currency, after the astronomical inflation and monetary disorganization of the civil war and the following years; and a reform in 1947 designed to mop up the excess consumer liquidity resulting from World War II. The revaluation of the ruble in terms of the dollar in 1961 was, however, of little practical significance. Fundamental credit reforms in 1930-32 put an end to the substantial circulation of trade bills and direct extension of interunit credits, and centralized practically all short-term credit activity in the Gosbank. Since then the credit system, though it has undergone further developments, has remained basically unchanged. There has been, however, a good deal of organizational restructuring of banking, reflecting the changes over the years in economic policy and organization and persistent efforts to tighten the Gosbank's control over payments flows.[1]

The development of Soviet financial arrangements has been hampered all along by adherence to theoretical views derived from the writings of Karl Marx, which relate to a capitalist financial environment of a century ago. The checkered history of the banking system over half a century of evolution can be viewed as a struggle to forge an effective tool for monitoring the fulfillment of economic plans and to preserve price stability by controlling payments flows. Although that system served as a model for all communist countries, the Soviet Union has lagged behind the others in the attempts to make money and credit play a more active part in the transformation of the economy away from a rigidly centralized form.

---

[1] *The history of developments before World War II is readily available in English; see A. Z. Arnold,* Banks, Credit, and Money in Soviet Russia *(New York: Columbia University Press, 1937).*

The standard system discussed in Part I is, in essence, the system originally developed in the Soviet Union. All that need be added in this chapter is a brief description of the evolution of its banking structure, of the modifications that have occurred in recent years, and of those that are currently under way.

THE BANKING SYSTEM

Since World War II there has been a strong tendency in the Soviet Union toward consolidation of banking institutions. Even before the war, notably in 1932 and 1936, various banks were consolidated that had been originally created to finance capital formation in specific economic sectors, including agriculture. Subsequently, in 1959, further mergers and reassignment of activities occurred, and as a result the Investment Bank (Stroibank) emerged as the single conduit of budgetary appropriations into fixed investment. And since the beginning of 1963 the savings bank system, with over 70,000 branches (including agencies in factories, offices, and farms), has been part of the Gosbank, operating as a separate department that is also in charge of selling government bonds.[2] Apart from the Gosbank and the Investment Bank, the only other banking institution now in existence is the Bank for Foreign Trade (Vneshtorgbank),[3] whose scope of operations was considerably increased in 1961. Originally, it was concerned mainly with currency exchange for tourists and diplomatic missions and with remittances, since payments for commercial transactions with foreigners were handled by the Gosbank. After its reorganization the Foreign Trade Bank has been handling all foreign settlements and also the crediting of foreign trade. Since the Investment Bank is essentially an administrative organization supervising the disbursement of government budget grants, and the Foreign Trade Bank is actually only a headquarters organization, the Gosbank is the purest example of a monobank, as it virtually alone services the cash, credit, and payments needs of a country with a population exceeding 230 million.

---

[2] *For descriptions of developments in savings banking, see A. G. Zverev,* Gosudarstvennye zaimy i vklady v sberegatel'nye kassy *(Government Loans and Savings Bank Deposits), Moscow, 1957,* G. Eremeeva, Razvitie sberegatel'nogo dela v SSSR *(The Development of Savings Banking in the USSR), Moscow, 1958, and A. Il'inich and G. Tkachenko,* Sberegatel'noe delo *(Savings Banking), Moscow, 1964.*

[3] *See M. Poliakov, "USSR Bank for Foreign Trade", E.G., February 29, 1964; English translation in* American Review of Soviet and Eastern European Foreign Trade, *No. 1, 1965.*

In its organization the Gosbank corresponds to the standard type of monobank described in Chapter 2. In addition to its policy-making head office *(pravlenie)* and its principal offices in the various republics, it has two levels (in some of the smaller republics, only one level) of regional offices *(raion)* and a network of about 3,500 local branches which are its main points of contact with enterprises, collective farms, and lower level government units. To service the urban population it maintains nearly 2,000 collection offices (originally part of the network of communal banks abolished in 1959), which receive payments for rent and service bills, taxes, and other compulsory payments and contributions. The office network also includes a small number (currently fewer than thirty) of special cash service agencies *(pripisnye kassy)* in large industrial establishments and construction projects. Seasonal agencies are operated at remote points where large purchases of farm products are made.

Little statistical information is available on the operations of the Gosbank. Its more than 150,000 employees service about 1.2 million clients: The bulk of all banking operations is with the approximately 250,000 enterprises that operate on the basis of cost accounting, or *khozraschet* (enterprises that have their own working capital, prepare a balance sheet and an income statement), and borrow regularly or occasionally. There are about 40,000 collective farm accounts. Nearly half a million are various government units and organizations (such as party, trade union, and cultural organizations) that have no access to credit. Most accounts held by individuals are loan accounts for home financing, which number around 400,000; in addition, there are a negligible number of individual savings deposits.

Aggregate balances maintained by Gosbank clients are small in comparison with cash balances held by business and government units in the United States. At the beginning of 1961, total balances in accounts of all *khozraschet* organizations amounted to less than 4.7 billion rubles[4] (compared with 3 billion rubles five years earlier), and all other current accounts came to only 1.6 billion rubles. It is not known how the sum of these two amounts (which corresponds approximately to demand deposits in the United States, including Treasury deposits at Federal Reserve and commercial banks) compares with note circulation data, as these are considered a state secret.

---

[4] *All amounts in this chapter are in post-1961 reform rubles.*

The operation of a centralized payments system poses many problems in a country the size of the Soviet Union, with its diverse economy and its comparatively small degree of industry integration. The system is based in the main on documentary drafts and involves processing a large number of items. In very recent years this operation has begun to be automated but the use of electronic equipment is still very limited.

The rapid increase in transactions by individuals—which has occurred even though consumer loans are extended by stores rather than by banks—has been a consequence of rising incomes, a rise in savings, provision of facilities for depositing wages in savings accounts and making periodic payments from them, and the growing importance of housing loans and of tourism. Since savings bank offices handle virtually all accounts and transactions of individuals, the great increase in these transactions seems to have been a main reason for the incorporation of the savings bank system into the Gosbank.

Of even greater importance as an operating problem has been the rise in transactions involving the collective farms. The relationship between the collective farms and the state, and between the farms and their members, began to be monetized in 1953. Under the system hitherto in force the collectives paid in kind for the services performed by the state-owned tractor and farm machinery stations, and had to deliver a large part of their output to the state at relatively low prices fixed by the government, which were in fact a form of taxation. In connection with the changes that started in 1953, the tractor and machinery stations were liquidated and their equipment was sold to the collectives. The farms then had to pay in cash for all machinery and fuel, as well as for building materials, fertilizer, and other supplies; on the other hand, they could sell their output to the state on contract, at significantly higher prices.

Since the early fifties, a gradual shift has been made toward remunerating members of collective farms in cash, rather than in kind, even though until recently they received their income annually, after the end of the crop year. In 1953 only one third of the compensation for work contributed by members was in cash; five years later the proportion had risen to more than half, and it was nearly three fourths in 1963. Since the beginning of 1965 the flow of money income to the farm population has been further increased by the introduction of state pension payments to the aged members of collective farms. The introduction in the summer of 1966 of minimum monthly payments to the members of collective farms will result in greater use of money in the farm sector.

The substantial growth of payments flows and bank lending in rural areas and the need to service an ever-growing clientele in villages have added to the complexity of Gosbank operations, traditionally geared to the needs of industry and government which are concentrated in urban areas. Thus the Gosbank has continuously attempted to simplify payments procedures. Efforts to speed up payments through local and industrywide compensation arrangements—whereby mutual claims were offset—have not been successful, and separate compensation offices were abolished in 1955. Other forms of compensation arrangements are now in effect, and local and regional offices have been experimenting on and off with a variety of procedures for accelerating payments, at least for certain categories of transactions.[5] Yet the Soviet banking and economic publications continue to devote much space to the need to improve the settlements mechanism, which seems to represent one of the major operating problems of the Gosbank.

The activities of the Gosbank are not limited to purely financial operations. Despite recent changes in other communist countries, the Soviet economy still does not provide the managers of enterprises with direct and powerful incentives or rewards for maximum performance. In fact, managers have no authority to innovate or even to make quite small modifications in established technology and procedures, as they are confronted with bureaucratic hurdles if they attempt any change, however small it may be. In such a system, a considerable part of improvements must be initiated by persons or organizations outside the enterprise. Ever since the creation of the Soviet regime, various techniques have been tried to provide such outside "assistance" for improving performance. In recent years the emphasis has shifted somewhat from party organs to "voluntary citizens' organizations" to serve this purpose, and "public bureaus of economic analysis" have been created at many enterprises and state farms. These organizations consist of several members of the enterprise staff who are directly engaged in production and administration (engineers, foremen, accountants) as well as economists from the various government agencies.[6] A large number of Gosbank economists are engaged in such "voluntary" activities in addition to their regular duties; in the Ukraine, for instance, at the beginning of 1965 there were nearly 5,000 bureaus,

[5] *I. Taflia, "Credit and the Acceleration of Settlements", D. K., January 1966. See also V. Babushkin, "Settlements and Costs", E. G., No. 36 (September 8, 1965), and A. Birman, "Do the Priority Payments Exist?", E. G., No. 38 (September 22, 1965).*

[6] *In Eastern Europe the word economist has a much broader connotation than in the West, in terms of both training and occupation; in all agencies concerned with the administration of economic activities, a large proportion of the professional staff are classified as economists.*

and more than 2,000 economists on the staffs of local and regional offices of the Gosbank participated in the work of these bureaus. Professional employees of the Gosbank also take active part in "voluntary" and auxiliary control organizations attached to the lower territorial units of the government and the party. In the words of an article in the bank's official publication:[7]

> Economists of the Gosbank are widely used by the control organs of the party and of the government to check the state of affairs in trade, in public eating places, in various establishments that service the population, and in the development of the network of movie theatres, and to conduct complex investigations of the business and financial activities of enterprises and organizations in the fields of production, trade, procurement, and other branches of the economy.

CREDIT PLANNING AND PRACTICES

Little need be added here to the discussion of planning in Chapter 4. Credit planning in the Soviet Union goes back to 1924, immediately after the introduction of a stable currency but several years before the extension of short-term credit became a monopoly of the Gosbank. The form and structure of the various monetary plans in use in the Soviet Union have changed little over time, but such changes as have taken place reflect in the main administrative changes rather than attempts at integration or at increasing the analytical value of the plans. In recent Soviet economic literature one encounters increasing recognition that financial planning involves more than mere balancing of accounting statements, and that the interrelationship of all financial accounts does not necessarily mean they are either integrated among themselves or consistent with the underlying physical balances. Some contemporary Soviet writers on banking subjects are aware of the need to extend financial analysis to deposit money, to the factors that determine the demand for such balances, and to money flows and velocity. So far, however, monetary planning has been limited, in effect, to currency circulation and, in view of the prevailing monetary arrangements, this is equivalent to saying it has been confined to the consumer sector.

Soviet economists have generally denied the monetary nature of bank deposits.

---

[7] I. Borzhanskaia, "On the Development of Social Principles in the Activity of the State Bank", D. K., August 1965, page 40.

Most of them consider such balances to be merely a settlement fund, a liability of the Gosbank, or a potential claim of the depositor to currency.[8] The relationship between credit and money creation is only dimly perceived, and the view is widely held that resources of the Gosbank determine its ability to expand credit. The "real bills" doctrine continues to be extolled, and great pains are taken to explain any departures as consistent with it. In Soviet monetary literature the relationship between the balance of international payments and domestic monetary equilibrium and money supply is generally ignored. Only recently a leading authority had to plead for recognition of the fact that the sale of foreign exchange proceeds by exporters, or their purchase by importers, may lead to a change in the volume of money in circulation.[9]

The heavy burden of orthodoxy is evident in the Gosbank's lending activities, which still follow the patterns described in Chapter 5. Since the end of the Stalin era there has been some tendency toward greater flexibility, but the bank's credit practices have been conservative and unimaginative when compared with those of most other communist countries. Until the announcement of more significant changes in the fall of 1965, progress was mainly in reducing the excessive compartmentalization of lending and in simplifying accounting procedures. Little was accomplished, even tentatively, toward using credit as a constructive tool for influencing the processes of production and distribution, rather than merely as an implementation of higher level decisions. It is difficult to say to what extent this lag vis-à-vis the other countries reflects a hesitancy resulting from the cumulative experience of disastrous effects from sudden and frequent changes in economic policy and organization, and how far it reflects a reluctance to give up monetary and credit theories that the Soviet Union itself has generated and elevated to the status of inviolability.

The present loan administration is a patchwork of procedures introduced to supplement the original system of gearing credit to financing the movement of real assets through the economic system. The proliferation of separate "objects of crediting", originally accompanied by the opening of a separate loan account (see Chapter 5), began almost with the establishment of the Gosbank: "produc-

---

[8] *An attempt by Professor Kronrod to have bank balances at least recognized as "money of the banking circuit" (the term "deposit money" apparently being avoided because of its capitalistic ancestry) met with widespread opposition.*

[9] *I. P. Aizenberg, "The Stability of Money in Domestic and External Circulation Under Socialism", D.K., November 1965.*

tion credit for specific purposes" made its appearance in the bank's balance sheet in 1922. Subsequently, whenever a new pressing need was identified, a new object of crediting was added. As a result, many items of small quantitative significance emerged in Gosbank statistics, including such entries as "loans for the construction of movie theatres". The trend toward compartmentalization of loans was not reversed until the midfifties. Since then the loan and current accounts of some enterprises have been merged, and various other simplifications that have increased the flexibility of credit administration have been adopted.[10] Credit on the basis of "norms" established for specific categories of inventories, with a specific ceiling for each, has now been replaced by loans for broad inventory categories, in most cases without specific upper limits. The more recent tendency toward crediting on the basis of total sales turnover makes funds available to pay for deliveries, as attested by shipping documents, with credit no longer being dependent on inspection reports based on actual visual checking of the level of inventories. In fact, this new method of crediting makes bank loans available for the financing of all production costs, including wages. At the beginning of 1965, however, still less than 11 per cent of total short-term credit outstanding in industry was on a turnover basis.

At the end of 1964, the latest year for which data are available, the total volume of short-term credit outstanding amounted to 63 billion rubles, compared with 17 billion rubles in 1950 (see Table 7). Loans directly secured by physical collateral accounted for three fourths of the 1964 total, and with the addition of credit documents in process of collection (covering goods shipped) the figure rises to over nine tenths, leaving less than 7 per cent for all other types of credit. These percentages are very close to those for the immediately preceding years, and not much different from the corresponding proportions at the end of 1950. The head of the credit department of the Gosbank does not expect this percentage to change materially even after the introduction of the new credit policies described below.[11]

Industry and retail trade each accounted for one third of the total volume of

[10] See T. Chernyshova's article, "The Unification of Forms and Methods of Short-term Lending", D.K., November 1964.

[11] See the article by N. Barkovskii, "On the Increased Role of Credit in the Economy", D.K., January 1966, page 21.

short-term credit outstanding at the end of 1964, and most of the remaining third was divided between wholesale trade and agriculture. More than 45 per cent of the short-term credit to industry, after subtracting the loans to finance collection float, was for carrying inventories of agricultural origin. Both cooperative and state farms are heavily dependent on credit, which currently meets about two thirds of all their production expenses apart from labor costs. Advance payments by state purchasing agencies account for a large part of the production credit extended to cooperatives, including (to the extent that the farms have shifted to the payment of money wages) the credit needed to finance the cost of labor.

TABLE 7

SHORT-TERM CREDIT OUTSTANDING IN THE USSR

	Year-end 1950	Year-end 1964
Total Outstanding (*in billions of rubles*)	**17.3**	**63.2**
By type of loan (*in per cent of total*)		
Secured by real assets	**62.5**	**74.7**
Raw materials and fuel	16.7	18.9
Goods in process	2.7	1.8
Finished goods	4.2	4.5
Construction equipment	0.9	1.8
Trade inventories	36.7	45.6
Wholesale trade	*6.5*	*7.6*
Procurement of farm products	*2.4*	*6.9*
Retail trade	*25.7*	*28.8*
Other inventories	*2.1*	*2.3*
Other real assets	1.3	2.1
Secured by items in process of collection	**28.8**	**18.8**
Other types of loans	**8.7**	**6.5**
By economic sector (*in per cent of total*)		
Industry	40.3	33.4
Agriculture (including collective farms)	3.3	6.7
Transportation and communications	1.3	0.8
Construction	3.5	4.8
Wholesale trade	14.9	12.0
Procurement of farm products	4.4	8.2
Retail trade	31.7	33.2
Other sectors	0.7	0.8

Source: Computed from Central Statistical Administration of the USSR, Narodnoe khoziaistvo SSSR v 1964 godu. Includes medium-term credit for technological improvements and for increasing the output of mass consumption goods.

TABLE 8

LONG-TERM CREDIT IN THE USSR, 1964

In millions of rubles

Type of loan	Outstanding at year-end	Loans granted during year
Loans to collective farms...............................	4,404	1,251
For construction of farm buildings......................		*412*
For equipment		*485*
For electrification		*85*
For other purposes.....................................		*269*
Loans to the population...............................	718	
Urban	289	
Rural	429	
Loans to state and cooperative enterprises and organizations	892	
Total	**6,014**	

Source: Central Statistical Administration of the USSR, Narodnoe khoziaistvo SSSR v 1964 godu.

A gradual shift toward direct Gosbank lending to the cooperatives—for labor as well as other costs—is now under way, as will be seen in the subsequent section.

Long-term credit has so far been available mainly to agriculture—where it is the main means of financing capital formation in collective farms—and for home construction. At the end of 1964 (see Table 8) the outstanding amount of such credit extended by the Gosbank and the Investment Bank, combined, was less than one tenth of the outstanding short-term loans, a proportion that has prevailed during most of the years since 1950. Certainly, the amount of credit extended to stimulate capital investment in agriculture is pitifully small in relation to needs. By the beginning of 1965, 2,700 new construction and building-material-producing enterprises had been created for the specific purpose of promoting the construction of farm buildings (particularly barns), but the aggregate amount of credit made available to them in the preceding year amounted to only 38.4 million rubles.[12] However, the total volume of long-term loans increased sharply in 1965, including credit to agriculture.

---

[12] *M. Maksimov, "The Bank and the Collective Farm Construction", D.K., November 1965.*

Since the early 1960's, Soviet credit administration has been gradually modified in some respects, and toward the end of 1965 a number of further changes were announced as a result of the Communist Party deliberations held in September and October. The proposed reforms represent, in effect, an adaptation of loan procedures to the new economic policy, which gives greater latitude to managers and aims at substituting economic incentives for administrative command. The reforms have been influenced by changes first introduced in Hungary in 1961, and to a certain degree in Poland, in connection with the reorientation of economic policies that followed the insurrectionary events of 1956. The new Soviet measures range over the Gosbank's entire field of activity, and represent new departures as well as measures to simplify and improve existing procedures, notably those pertaining to the payments mechanism and credit sanctions.[13] Of particular importance for the future activities of the banking system is a move away from budget financing, at least as regards investment projects with a relatively short recoupment period.

Various measures have been taken to alleviate the credit burden on agriculture which, it is admitted, has resulted to a considerable degree from policies now considered faulty. About 1.5 billion rubles of collective farms' long-term debt, and over half a billion of their short-term debt, have been written off; and other obligations too have been canceled or postponed. Farm production credit will become available directly from the Gosbank instead of through advances of state purchasing agencies. This shift to direct lending by the Gosbank entails large-scale experimentation with alternative methods of crediting, involving about 3,000 collective farms that differ in size, profitability, and location.[14]

Moreover, in an attempt to encourage individual initiative where state and collective farms have conspicuously failed, credit is now being made available to increase ownership of cattle. For a loan to buy a cow—the maximum loan amount is 300 rubles for one cow per family, or 150 rubles for a calf—a request must be addressed to the state or collective farm, or in rural or suburban areas where cattle can be raised as a sideline by urban workers, to the enterprise or government unit where the individual is employed. The employer—administrative official

---

[13] See "Methodical Directives", E.G., No. 6 (February 1966), pages 31-35.

[14] Credit at the Service of Collective Farm Production", interview with A. A. Poskonov, head of the Gosbank, E.G., No. 2 (January 1966), page 38.

of the farm or general manager of the enterprise—decides whether the loan should be granted, and then submits the application to the appropriate bank office. The employer guarantees the loan, acts as collection agent for the bank by withholding the amounts needed for monthly amortization and for interest payment (2 per cent annually), makes sure that the proceeds are actually spent for the stated purpose, and collects the balance due if the animal is sold or slaughtered. These procedures are typical of the bureaucratic handicaps involved in the extension of credit to individuals and the terms—including the amortization over a period of seven years, after one year of grace to repay a $330 loan— reflect the low level of incomes.

In an effort to encourage the manufacture of new products and improved models, loans will become available to acquire raw materials and carry goods in process above the levels stipulated in the original plans. Experiments are under way for extending credit on a global basis, rather than for designated purposes and with specific collateral, and for letting the individual enterprise use these funds at its discretion, without detailed planning and control by the Gosbank. In an endeavor to prevent working capital from being impaired because of buyers' failure to meet obligations on time, loans of up to thirty days are to be made available to pay suppliers; such loans are to be repaid in the same order of preference as those secured by real assets.

Other changes in credit practices, such as introduction of lending on the basis of total turnover, are designed to reduce the required "documentation"— detailed verifications and other paperwork—and to provide greater flexibility in the use of borrowed funds in accordance with changing needs.

In connection with the greater latitude permitted to plant managers, there will be a reduction in the role of the authorities interposed between the individual enterprise and the relevant ministry. Thus enterprises will themselves determine their working-capital requirements, and these requirements, once approved by the higher echelon authorities, cannot be changed during the year, unless the production plan is modified. As a result, the higher level authority will no longer be able to take away or transfer to some other enterprise working capital that it judges to be excessive. For enterprises whose working capital has been impaired because of losses or less-than-projected profits, the shortfall will no longer be made good through budgetary appropriations but will have to be rebuilt from future profits.

The partial shift to loan financing of fixed capital formation has been under discussion at least since 1957, with the old guard arguing that it would weaken planning.[15] The present plans call for gradual moves. Enterprise managers will have more independence in determining plans and financing plant expansion, modernization, and repair. The individual enterprises will accumulate resources for such expenditures in "funds for the development of production"—constituted from retained earnings, part of depreciation allowances, and the sale of redundant equipment and miscellaneous sources—to be used primarily for the improvement of technology; in some cases, industrywide investment funds will be formed from part of these resources. Whatever additional investment funds the enterprise may require will be supplied on a repayable credit basis by the Investment Bank, which has recently been doing this on a limited experimental basis, provided the loan can be amortized within six years from the time the new facility begins to operate. Even entirely new factories will receive Investment Bank financing if the loan can be retired within a relatively small number of years from the projected cash flow of the new plant. Only projects for which the internal flow of funds will not permit full loan retirement within six years will continue to be financed through budget grants, and each such allocation will require the approval of the Council of Ministers. For some time, however, budgetary financing will continue to be important; over the next several years, self-financed investment in industry is not expected to exceed 20 per cent of the total, and apparently considerable differences of opinion exist with regard to the proportion of total investment which should or, in effect, will be financed through loans.

In combination with the partial shift from budget to loan financing, there will be a charge—for the benefit of the budget—on the fixed and working capital of enterprises, in order to equalize the cost of using new and existing investment.[16] The role of the Gosbank in financing fixed investment will not be increased significantly, but there will be a liberalization of the conditions on which it makes loans for new and improved technology and for enlarging the production of mass consumption goods. One half of the turnover tax levied on consumer goods, instead of being channeled into the budget, will be used as a source of funds for loan repayment.

---

[15] *See, for instance, K. Plotnikov, "Certain Problems of the Development of Finance and Credit in the Building of Communism", Voprosy* Ekonomiki, *October 1964, English translation of which appeared in* Problems of Economics, *February 1965. See also Barkovskii's article cited in footnote 11.*

[16] *See the "Provisional Directive Concerning Payments into the Budget for Fixed and Working Capital", E.G., No. 17 (April 1966), page 32, and V. Bocharov, "On the Differentiation of Charges on Capital",* Planovoe Khoziaistvo, *May 1966, pages 63-69.*

134

One of the ideological hurdles that Soviet officials have great difficulty in overcoming is the role of interest in allocating resources. As one of the vice chairmen of the Gosbank wrote recently, "Up to now, interest rates and their differentiation did not result in any serious influence on the economic and financial activity of enterprises".[17] Practically uniform interest rates on short-term credit still prevail, with higher rates automatically charged as a penalty for overdue loans.

Interest has not played a significant role since the credit reforms of 1930-32. Until then, rates were as high as 8 per cent, and were differentiated according to purpose and maturity (though not the financial condition of the borrower). Under the system that has been in existence for the last thirty-five years, virtually uniform rates are applied to all short-term loans, irrespective of borrower or purpose, with interest serving mainly the purpose of raising enough revenue to cover the expenses of the Gosbank. Loans to facilitate settlements carry a nominal rate of 1 per cent, and on all other short-term loans the annual charge is 2 per cent. For overdue loans there is a penalty rate of 3 per cent to collective farms, 5 per cent to all other economic enterprises. The several distinct purposes for which long-term loans can be obtained carry annual interest charges ranging from 3/4 of 1 per cent to 2 per cent. It is not yet clear how much interest rates will be differentiated in the future, this being one of the major issues still unresolved, but the principle has been established that bank funds should be more expensive than the charge on "own" working capital, and that borrowing made necessary by management shortcomings (excessive inventories, for example, or impaired working capital) should carry higher rates than loans to finance normal needs. It appears that penalty rates for overdue loans and for late payments will be increased and their collection more vigorously enforced. The levels at which rates on loans for investment purposes and equivalent charges on existing capital are to be set are still under discussion.

The changes announced in the fall of 1965 not only will require considerable modification in the old systems and procedures of financial planning, settlements, accounting, and control,[18] but will also entail substantial internal reorganization, increase in the scope of the activities of lower echelon offices (hitherto confined largely to putting into effect instructions received from above), and

---

[17] V. Karabekov, "Credit and Production", E.G., No. 52 (December 1965) ,page 7.

[18] For instance, control over expenditures for wages and salaries is to be exercised on a quarterly basis instead of on the basis of five- or ten-day periods, as in the past.

more importantly a change in the thinking and attitude of the Gosbank operating staffs. Up to now, according to the official publication of the Gosbank, many of the bank's territorial offices "have proceeded by bureaucratic rote and have regarded paperwork and the issuance of innumerable instructions, orders, and regulations as their basic method of exercising leadership".[19] The head of the Gosbank, in discussing the implications of the new policies, is quoted as commenting that the bank must now "free itself from imposing tutelage down to minute details on economic units, and from administrative forms and methods of dealing with the economy, and give as much scope as possible to the action of economic and material stimulants".[20]

The specific measures to implement the new policies are now being worked out in detail. A first step has already been made to provide credit on the new basis to the first group of enterprises which have been experimentally shifted to the new system of management at the beginning of 1966. If and when the new policies are fully put into effect, the resulting changes will add up to the most significant development in the Soviet credit system since the reforms of 1930-32. The success of these changes will depend, in the last analysis, on the further development of the recently initiated changes in economic policy.

10. Poland

Poland's entire banking and monetary system was disorganized during the war, when Germany annexed parts of the country. The Provisional Government in 1945 created a new central bank, the National Bank of Poland (Narodowy Bank Polski—NBP), and at the same time reactivated the major prewar state-owned commercial banks. These banks engaged in a wide range of credit operations, but mostly discounted commercial paper (self-liquidating loans for

---

[19] *To Increase Economic Stimulation of Industrial Output"*, D.K., *November 1965, page 13.*

[20] *"Let us Put into Practice the Decisions of the September Plenum of the Central Committee of the Communist Party of the Soviet Union"*, D.K., *November 1965, page 93.*

productive purposes) for both the socialized and the private sectors of the economy. In the first postwar years the NBP, while fulfilling the functions of a bankers' bank and rediscounting a large part of the portfolios of the commercial banks, also engaged in direct lending. But it lacked broad policy instruments that could have enabled it to control effectively the aggregate volume of credit— a task which, in any case, faced great difficulties in a country attempting to reconstruct its economy after wartime devastation and distortions and at the same time incorporating large new territories in the West.

After a reorganization of the banking system in 1948, the NBP assumed the character of a monobank. By that time, discounted commercial paper had shrunk to 2 per cent of the bank's total loan portfolio, and the NBP was granting credit on the basis of the principles developed in the Soviet Union, gradually extending financial controls over its borrowers. The commercial banks were in process of liquidation, and in 1950 their remaining activities were transferred to the mono- bank. Meanwhile, a series of measures made it mandatory that payments within the socialized sector be effected by deposit transfer. Long-term lending and the administration of budgetary grants for investment were made the responsibility of the Investment Bank (Bank Inwestycyjny, subordinated to the Ministry of Finance), and the task of financing agriculture was given to the Agricultural Bank (Bank Rolny). In addition to the NBP, the Investment Bank and the Agricultural Bank have a fairly extensive network of local offices. The Com- mercial Bank (Bank Handlowy w Warszawie), operating under the charter of an old commercial bank established in 1870, was originally put in charge of banking services related to trade with the West. Since 1964 its status has been that of a foreign trade bank, handling foreign payments of all Polish import and export organizations throughout the world. Since early 1964 the Foreign Depart- ment of the NBP discontinued handling foreign trade payments by transferring these activities and the related bank connections to the Commercial Bank, which is currently planning to establish several branches abroad.

The banking reorganizations of 1948 and 1950 gave the banking system of Poland a closer resemblance to that of the Soviet Union, even in such details as making short-term lending to the construction industry and to collective farms a responsibility of the institutions that administered long-term credit in these two sectors. In contrast to the Soviet Union, however, a large network of rural loan and savings cooperatives was preserved mainly to service the large private sector in agriculture. The prewar postal savings system—now operating under the name of General Savings Bank (Powszechna Kasa Oszczędności)—was reorganized and entrusted with the performance of certain banking services. It has nearly 200 offices located in the principal cities, and it also maintains agencies at more than 6,500 post offices, thus making its facilities available to the smallest villages.

To attract the largest possible amount of remittances from the Polish emigrants throughout the world, the activities of a special bank, known abroad as the Bank Pekao (Bank Polska Kasa Opieki), were broadened after 1956. It opened branches in the principal Polish cities, and a network of stores was created in which nationals can acquire consumer goods—and also farm implements and equipment for repair shops and other small enterprises left in private hands— by paying in foreign exchange remitted by relatives and friends abroad. The bank has branches in Paris and Tel Aviv, which operate as full-fledged commercial banks, and affiliates in New York and Toronto, which are organized as commercial trading companies and merely accept orders for delivery of merchandise packages in Poland.

The network of credit cooperatives was reconstituted in 1957, replacing the formerly existing system of rural savings banks that provided banking facilities exclusively for farmers. Credit cooperatives are located in both rural and urban areas and are supervised by a central organization (Association of Savings and Loan Cooperatives). They extend credit not only to individual farmers and to members of farm cooperatives, but also to craftsmen and other independent producers and to the population in general. They accept deposits from their members, have limited borrowing facilities at the Agricultural Bank and the NBP, and represent a main source of credit for private entrepreneurs. Resources available to the cooperatives for lending to agriculture are augmented each year by special allocations of funds from the budget. In addition, mutual-aid banks of production cooperatives and housing cooperatives accept savings deposits from their members. The network of credit unions is sponsored by trade union locals and attached to the various places of employment. They pay no interest on deposits but make no charges on consumer loans advanced to their members; they also issue "trade union vouchers", financed from a government loan, which are accepted by stores in lieu of cash.

Since 1953 the NBP has been the source of about 90 per cent of all short-term credit to the economy, financing about half of the inventories held and more than half of the payments in process of collection. In the fifties, nearly all short-term loans went to the socialized sector, but since 1959 the share of the private sector —in the main, agriculture—has increased. The operations of the communist credit system have experienced more difficulties in Poland than in any other country of Eastern Europe, partly because of chronic overspending of the wages fund and the excessive accumulation of inventories.

There was considerable public debate during 1956-58 on the need to make sweeping changes in the credit system. A new statute enacted in 1958 made few fundamental changes—it states explicitly that the NBP "carries out the monetary and credit policy of the state according to the direction of the Minister of Finance"—but it brought about some noteworthy modifications. In line with other changes in the Polish economy, more emphasis was placed on the financial independence of enterprises, including retention of a greater part of profits to finance fixed- and working-capital needs. At the same time, the flexibility of bank offices in making loans was considerably increased. Reliance on controlling the end use of credit through the proliferation of "objects of crediting" was largely abandoned by reducing them to one third of the number in use between 1952 and 1958. In most instances, credit extended for specific purposes was replaced by lending on total turnover, which by the midfifties became the general method of extending credit to industry as well as to trade. As in Hungary, a year earlier, enterprises were given the right to determine their own working-capital requirements (norms). They were given access to bank credit for the amounts by which these norms exceeded their internal funds, but the bank could refuse credit if it judged the norms to be excessive. The rigid priorities for making payments from enterprise accounts were abolished.

In addition, the 1958 reforms gave enterprises limited access to long-term credit for decentralized investments (normally up to five years and in special cases up to ten years) and reduced administrative controls over their current accounts at the NBP. The interest rate charged, originally calculated only to cover operating costs of the NBP, was made flexible, and the bank's power to apply sanctions against poorly performing borrowers was increased. Thus the NBP now can charge as high as 12 per cent for overdue working-capital loans, and as low as 1 per cent for loans to finance investments and for other purposes judged to be in the interest of the national economy. Managers of branch offices have acquired in recent years considerable latitude in fixing interest rates on individual loans.

The decentralization of capital formation has already made considerable progress in Poland as compared with the late fifties, when enterprises were responsible for only about 2 per cent of all investments in industry, but non-repayable budgetary grants still account for about two thirds of the total. Further steps to increase decentralized investments are envisaged for the future. The portion of profits and depreciation reserves retained by individual plants will be increased, and the proportion of fixed investment financed by industry associations (rather than by the national authorities), which in recent years has ranged between 17 per cent and 19 per cent, is to be doubled. Credit still plays only a small part in the financing of fixed capital formation in industry—on the order of 2 per cent.

To encourage maximum economies in the use of working capital, the 1958 system of theoretical norms established by the enterprises themselves is now being abolished. Henceforth, the percentage of "own" funds and of bank loans in the total volume of working capital actually in use in a given industry will be determined by that industry. The individual enterprise must maintain the prescribed percentage of own resources in its share of the industry's total working capital. If its resources are insufficient for this, it can obtain funds from the bank at rates higher than those applicable to the proportion normally provided by credit. Such loans must be retired from future increases in internal funds before the increases can be used for any other purposes, such as investment projects initiated by the enterprise itself. Any economies in the amount of working capital actually in use will augment the volume of funds available for fixed investment by the enterprise. Financing needs arising from overstocking will also be met by bank credit, granted at higher rates, however. Keeping inventories at low levels is to be further encouraged by paying interest on balances left on deposit with the bank.

In view of the concealed and open unemployment that exists in certain areas and in certain categories of labor, special credit facilities ("intervention funds") have been made available recently to stimulate private and cooperative initiative in creating jobs where this problem is particularly acute.

A distinguishing characteristic of the Polish system is that the volume of credit to individual farmers exceeds loans to farm cooperatives, since independent farms represent the overwhelming bulk of agriculture. Prior to 1957, farmers who owned more than 100 acres had no access to credit, but this exclusion of the large farmers is no longer practiced. At the end of 1964 the amount of outstanding bank credit (including that granted by savings and credit cooperative societies) to individual farmers—embracing also individual members of cooperative farms, farm laborers, and agriculture associations—was more than ten times as large as the amount outstanding to cooperative farms; this was true for short-term as well as long-term credit.

Poland also pioneered among communist countries in making credit available for the construction of cooperative and individual housing (with maturities up to forty years); such units now account for a fairly large amount of total residential construction (nearly 30 per cent in 1958). And Poland was the first communist country to introduce consumer credit on a large scale—since 1960, even in rural communities. Savings and loan cooperatives are used as the financing agent; they provide consumers with cash to pay the retail store up to 80 per cent of the purchase price, and collect instalment payments which can run up to eighteen months.

The system of financial planning is perhaps even more elaborate in Poland than in the Soviet Union, including, for instance, a separate plan for the insurance sector. An aggregate financial plan is prepared for the state enterprise sector. There is more publicity than elsewhere concerning the structure of the various financial plans—with actual figures published occasionally—and considerable public discussion of their analytical significance.

The new investment policies now being introduced are part of a major overhaul of the entire system of economic planning and management in which the profit ratio is being elevated to the position of the key success indicator.[1] Another basic ingredient in the new system is increased price flexibility, but the principle of centralized setting of prices for basic raw materials is still adhered to. The chief planner of the country, S. Jedrychowsky, has said that "the socialist economy cannot do without using prices as an important instrument for shaping supply and demand", but only the future can tell whether there will be a radical revision of pricing policies. The recent halfway move toward market allocation of resources through a flexible price system requires considerable ingenuity in administration, and burdens the banking system with decisions that would not be required with a properly functioning price mechanism. For instance, at the end of 1965 it was announced that the Ministry of Domestic Trade will henceforth prepare, every six months, lists of consumer goods for which supply exceeds demand and lists of those for which supplies are deficient. Only enterprises from the second list can now obtain credit for wage payments, if such payments exceed the amounts stipulated in the applicable plan.

[1] See Alexander Paszyńsky, "The New Model", Polish Perspectives, October 1965, and Thad P. Alton, "Polish Industrial Planning", Journal of International Affairs, No. 1, 1966.

Rumania suffered considerably less destruction of real capital during World War II than most other countries of Eastern Europe. Like its neighbors, however, it went through a postwar period of inflation and general shortages of goods, as production and trade had declined to less than half of the prewar level. At the end of 1946, even before the proclamation of the People's Republic and the subsequent dissolution of political parties or their absorption into the Workers' (Communist) Party, the central bank was nationalized. In contrast to the procedure in other communist countries, its owners were paid a compensation, based on the value of shares as quoted on the stock exchange on the day of nationalization. Under its new name of State Bank (Banca de Stat), the nationalized institution—which was to revert to its traditional name of National Bank in 1965—began immediately to exercise control over credit activities of the commercial banks.

Basic political and economic transformations were effected in 1948. A currency reform, including the creation of a new monetary unit, was instituted to absorb the overhang of war-generated currency; the commercial banks were nationalized, along with the bulk of all nonfarm establishments; the "popular banks" were transformed into consumer and producer cooperatives. In this process the Banca de Stat assumed the functions of a monobank. Until 1959, when the first significant changes in credit administration were undertaken, the Rumanian credit and banking system resembled very closely its Soviet prototype. There are many similarities between the unfolding of events in Rumania and in neighboring Hungary.

In addition to the National Bank, the banking system of Rumania at present includes only the Investment Bank, subordinated to the Ministry of Finance, and a network of savings banks. The Agricultural Bank, formed in 1954, was liquidated at the end of 1960, its functions being assigned to the State and the Investment Banks. At the same time, the cooperative farm credit societies, which numbered about 1,200 and operated in effect as local branches of the Agricultural Bank, were made part of the savings bank system, as most farm properties had by then been absorbed into collective farms.

The savings bank network of offices is widespread, including 15,000 limited agencies in factories, offices, state farms, and elsewhere; in addition to accepting deposits, the savings banks afford limited deposit transfer facilities to the population. In contrast to most of the other countries, the savings bank system has a very limited active business. Prior to 1961 it was merely a conduit for channeling private savings into the budget and for placing general government loans and a variety of lottery loans. After the absorption in that year of the farm credit cooperatives, it began to extend short-term loans to independent (noncollectivized) farmers on the basis of delivery contracts concluded with government purchasing agencies for farm products.

The Investment Bank, which was created in 1948, not only fulfills the usual functions of such a bank in disbursing budgetary funds earmarked for investment, but also engages in long-term lending to producer and consumer cooperatives and to individuals and cooperatives for residential building, and now also makes loans for small-scale technological improvements.

The credit reform of 1959 simplified both planning and procedures. The number of "objects of crediting" was reduced from at least thirteen to eight, and most credit, up to stipulated limits, is now extended almost automatically. The State Bank's quarterly credit plan is now prepared with direct participation of enterprises; a distinguishing aspect is the use of graphical cash flow analysis to project credit needs (and to control the flow of receipts and expenditures). The "own" funds of enterprises (except in trade) are now set at a level calculated to cover normal needs in the quarter with the lowest level of activity, and credit is used mostly for seasonal needs. In recent years, several measures have been taken to increase to about 50 per cent the proportion of bank credit in total working capital, partly in order to increase bank control over its use.

One distinctive Rumanian development is the channeling of enterprise payments flows through two strictly separate accounts, an arrangement that was introduced in 1958 on an experimental basis and generally instituted in 1959. All sales receipts are credited to "Account B", but the amounts needed to cover direct production costs are immediately transferred to "Account A", from which all payments for wages and materials are made. In addition, all short-term loans are credited to and repaid from this account. The funds that remain in Account B serve to make payments into amortization reserves and other special funds and to pay taxes, profits, and other accounts due to the government. These various payments are made at quite frequent intervals, but funds that accumulate in Account B can be used to replenish temporarily working capital in Account A and thus reduce the need for bank credit.

Rumania pioneered with the introduction of reserve funds from which loans could be made to enterprises in need of temporary assistance. These funds are at the disposal of central administrations and ministries for lending to enterprises under their supervision, thus bypassing the State Bank and its controls. Originally the reserve funds were formed by transferring to them a fixed proportion—13 per cent—of the working capital of each enterprise. Reforms in 1961 made these contributions more flexible by reducing the proportion of working capital transferred and adding resources derived from better-than-planned profits and from working capital considered excessive by the enterprises themselves. Under the new rules the reserve funds are used not only for credits to enterprises—now limited to ninety days—but also for reimbursing the National Bank for defaults on loans guaranteed by the central administrations and ministries.

Since the abolition of the Agricultural Bank in 1960, all short- and long-term credit to farm cooperatives has been extended by the National Bank. Cooperative farms work more than four fifths of Rumania's arable land, and in view of the important role of agriculture in the economy, financing of capital investment is an important part of the National Bank's activity. Loans for up to fifteen years are available for a variety of purposes, including acquisitions of cattle and farm machinery. From 1960 to 1964, long-term credits to farm cooperatives financed about one third of their investment in capital goods and livestock, and bank credit accounted for about half of all the funds available to state farms. Long-term credit is available also to the individual farmers, who are to be found mainly in the mountainous and other less productive areas. Individual farmers, however, pay a higher interest rate (7 per cent) than members of farm cooperatives (2 per cent), and for all practical purposes they must contract with government purchasing organizations for a large part of their production as the precondition for obtaining loans. For the construction of farm houses, loans are available to all categories of farmers at the nominal rate of 0.1 per cent per annum.

Credit at the same low cost is available through the Investment Bank for urban residential construction by individuals and for cooperative housing, provided the prospective builder is able to finance 10 per cent of construction costs with his own funds. The amounts of such loans are fixed for various categories of residential units to be constructed, and amortization periods are also rigidly established for each category. A penalty rate of 4 per cent is charged for payments overdue, and 12 per cent is levied on funds spent for purposes other than those originally approved. Lending for the introduction of new technology, small-scale mechanization, and stimulation of the mass production of consumer goods was introduced in 1954, but a decade later the volume of such credit was still quite modest. In 1963, repayment terms for these loans were lengthened and the rate charged was reduced to 1 per cent.

12. East Germany
(German Democratic Republic)

In East as in West Germany the groundwork for the banking system now in existence was laid by the occupation authorities. The Russian military government promptly liquidated the offices of the Reichsbank and all large commercial banks in the territory it administered,[1] and a network of new publicly owned institutions was created in the various administrative units of the Russian occupation zone. Savings banks and credit cooperatives, which were quite important in prewar Germany, were put under the control of the Russian military government.

The new banking system began to take shape in 1948, over a year before the October 1949 proclamation of the "German Democratic Republic". In 1948 the various regional banks that had been established by the occupation authorities were centralized under the Deutsche Emissions - und Girobank, which was later renamed the Deutsche Notenbank (bank of issue); an Investment Bank was created; and a new currency unit was introduced (now known as the *Mark der Deutschen Notenbank,* or MDN). By the early 1950's the banking system in essentially its present form was operating strictly along the lines of the Soviet blueprint, with the Notenbank having all the functions of a monobank.

The present system includes, in addition to the Notenbank and the Investment Bank, the usual specialized banking institutions: that for agriculture, the Landwirtschaftsbank, was organized in 1950 as the Deutsche Bauernbank (its name being changed in 1963) into which the independent regional farm banks were merged in 1952; that for foreign trade, the Deutsche Aussenhandelsbank, which started its operations in July 1966 and which apparently is the successor to the Handelsbank, created in 1956 in East Berlin. A distinctive characteristic of the East German banking scene is a network of about 230 cooperative banks for artisans (Banken für Handwerk und Gewerbe). These remnants of a formerly much larger number of such cooperatives are managed by their members, although supervised by the Notenbank, and have the function of providing credit and banking facilities to small producers and traders in the private sector. There also exists a widespread network of about 3,150 farm credit cooperatives, the

---

[1] *Some small banks in the part originally occupied by United States troops were not closed down until 1953. Only one small private bank is still in existence, in Leipzig.*

outcome of an amalgamation of the prewar Raiffeisenkassen with other organizations created to mold East German agriculture in the Soviet image; they combine farm lending with other activities, including cooperative purchases of supplies and sales of produce. In contrast to other countries of Eastern Europe, savings banks operate in East Germany under primarily local authority, rather than as a single nationwide network. Each of the 125 savings banks (more than 5,000 branches) is subordinate to its local political administration, though since 1956 the entire network has been under the general supervision of the Ministry of Finance. There is, in addition, a nationwide postal savings system, operating through more than 11,000 post offices, and even a separate savings bank for the railway system.

Another peculiarity of the East German system—one that arises from the special position of Berlin—is the Berliner Stadtkontor, a separate banking institution, which was created in the Russian sector in July 1945 almost immediately after the end of hostilities and which now operates, in effect, as the East Berlin branch of the Notenbank. Similarly, the Volksbank (People's Bank) serves substantially as the East Berlin counterpart of the banks for artisans.

The Notenbank is administered by a seven-man board of directors (Direktorium). Its president is a member of the Council of Ministers and of the Collegium of the Finance Ministry. Originally the bank was subordinated to the Ministry of Finance, which is in charge of preparing the overall credit plan, but by a law of December 20, 1965 it was placed under the Council of Ministers. This law defines the position and the tasks of the bank within the "new economic system for the planning and management of the national economy", which is currently being promulgated in East Germany. It explicitly authorizes the bank to use credit and interest for the achievement of economic goals and for maintaining internal stability of the currency. The law empowers the president of the Notenbank to set and apply differential rates of interest in accordance with economic requirements and the general policy determined by the Council of Ministers.

In East Germany a private sector, though it is small and steadily shrinking, still exists in industry and trade as well as in agriculture. Because of the survival of this sector the Notenbank has the distinctive feature among monobanks of carrying the accounts of some private firms and farmers, thereby providing a means of government supervision over their payments. All private firms that employ ten persons or more, and all farmers who own more than twenty hectares (almost fifty acres) must keep their current accounts with the Notenbank. The smaller private firms and farmers, like other private individuals, can have deposit accounts in the cooperative banks for artisans, in savings banks, or in the postal savings system.

Formerly, loans to agriculture were extended by the Notenbank or by the Investment Bank, depending on the maturity of the credits, but since 1958 financing of agriculture has been concentrated in the Landwirtschaftsbank. The latter serves as a "sector bank", meeting both short-term and long-term credit needs. It makes long-term loans for the purchase of cattle, farm machinery, and so on, and—with mortgages as security—for the construction of homes and the reconstruction of destroyed or war-damaged farms. It also extends credit to the large independent farmers (those who own more than twenty hectares) and accepts deposits from them. Furthermore, it lends to farm credit cooperatives, which are the source of credit for the small farmers, and to rural consumer cooperatives. The amount of short-term credit available to individual farmers (calculated as a percentage of the value of contractual deliveries to the state) is scaled down as the size of the farm increases, and the same principle applies to long-term loans. In making agricultural credit available, East Germany has consistently attempted to reduce the importance of the larger farmers, considered to be inimical to the regime, and to impose a transformation of agriculture after the Soviet model. Since the 1960 drive to bring farmers into collectives, the number of independent farmers has been sharply reduced, and most lending in the agricultural sector is now to collective farms.

Savings banks hold about three fourths of all savings deposits, but such accounts are available also at the Landwirtschaftsbank, the banks for artisans, the farm credit cooperatives, and the postal savings system. Both the savings banks and the postal savings system offer facilities for the transfer of personal funds. Not only is the network of offices at which savings accounts are available to the population particularly widespread, but the savings banks of East Germany seem to make special efforts to attract a maximum of funds by offering a choice between a variety of accounts.

Credit practices differ in some respects from those of the other communist countries. On the one hand, East Germany has clearly had great difficulty—connected with the continuous problems its economy has encountered—in adhering to the Soviet principles of credit planning and policy. Throughout the fifties there was a large volume of overdue loans, and special arrangements had to be made to carry "unplanned" inventories, consisting partly of goods that were of poor quality or for other reasons unsalable. The Notenbank's right to apply credit sanctions was widened significantly only in 1959, when maximum penalty rates for overdue loans were also raised sharply.

On the other hand, the Notenbank has been somewhat more flexible and imaginative than its counterparts in the neighboring countries. For instance, it goes further in extending credit without prior establishment of specific credit lines, particularly in trade. Since 1958 it has extended "liquidity credits" (*Liquiditätskredite*) to government enterprises, enabling them to rebuild working capital depleted by losses and to meet such current expenditures as fringe benefits to the staff (the so-called fund for social and cultural needs) and wage and salary bonuses for exceptional performance. Such loans, which take the place of replenishments from the national budget, are extended without collateral for a period of up to one year (but with a stiff penalty rate of 8 per cent for overdue loans). Short-term credit is made available also to private producers and traders, up to a fairly low maximum amount, and to joint (public-private) enterprises. The share of the private sector in total short-term credit declined from 22.5 per cent in 1949 to 2.6 per cent in 1959, but it is still larger than in other communist countries.

Although investment is normally financed from budgetary funds, distributed as grants by the Investment Bank, the allocation of such funds has since 1955 been dependent on the enterprises' meeting their planned targets, particularly with regard to profits and the payment of the stipulated proportion of profits and amortization funds into the budget. Long-term investment credits for stimulating production of mass consumption and export goods were also introduced in 1955, and in 1957 such credits became available for various kinds of investments designed to increase productivity (automation, for instance) and to broaden the range of goods produced. The responsibility for extending these long-term credits was given to the Notenbank, because it has a wider network of branches than the Investment Bank. In 1959, four years after investment credits were introduced, they accounted for only 4 per cent of all capital investment in state-owned industry. The Investment Bank makes investment credit available also to the private sector, either directly or (up to MDN 20,000) through the intermediary of the banks for artisans. Those artisans who are not members of such banks can obtain long-term credit from savings banks.

During 1964, radical changes were introduced in credit policy and banking organization. Much greater responsibility was given to the eighty-two associations, consisting of some 1,800 enterprises, which are directly responsible for two thirds of industrial output. So-called Industrie-Bankfilialen, or Industriebanken, were created as special branches of the Notenbank, each of them serving as a specialized industry bank for up to three of the associations. Although the annual credit plan of the Notenbank must still be approved by the Council of Ministers, the individual enterprises now draft their own quarterly plans. The General Director of the association to which the enterprises belong approves or modifies these quarterly plans. After aggregating them, he adds the association's requirements and submits the result to the relevant Industriebank for final approval. The plan he submits includes an industrywide contingency reserve, which is at the disposition not of the bank but rather of the General Director, whereby special loans may be made available to enterprises that require resources in excess of those provided in the plan.

The 1964 reforms produced important changes also in investment financing. Hitherto, enterprise management had planning responsibility for investment projects up to MDN 1 million (about $450,000 at the official, highly overvalued exchange rate), but all larger projects had to be planned by higher level authorities (by the Council of Ministers if the project cost exceeded MDN 5 million). At present, the enterprise manager and the General Director of the association have increased authority in planning fixed investment, and its financing is conducted more often through internal funds and credit than, as formerly, through budget grants. The difference between the unit's available internal resources and the cost of the project is financed through a bank loan, with the repayment schedule calculated to permit debt service and amortization out of the flow of retained profits and depreciation allowances. Financing of construction and equipment until the project becomes operative is now the responsibility of contractors and suppliers, whose own working capital is supplemented by short-term bank loans. Interest charges are used as a means of promoting completion of the project within the planned period, with penalty rates becoming effective after the agreed-upon completion date. Special resources available to the associations for investment purposes provide increased flexibility in planning and financing, and make it possible to draw up long-term investment plans.

The new desire for flexibility is evident also in the provisions regarding working-capital loans. As before, the amount and specific purpose of credit extended must conform with the objectives of the economic plan, but certain terms must be negotiated between bank and borrower. Since mid-1964 this agreement has had to be embodied in a "credit contract", a legal document that specifically defines the obligations of the borrower and the rights of the lender and simplifies the bank's control functions. Here too the greater responsibility of the associations should result in greater independence from centralized controls and a good deal of maneuverability in using economic levers.

13. Czechoslovakia

Czechoslovakia suffered relatively little destruction of capital and human resources during World War II. In 1948, when it became a "People's Republic", it was one of the two most industrially developed countries of Eastern Europe. Its monetary and banking system, however, had been disorganized by the creation of new institutions in the areas annexed by Germany and Hungary, by the amputation of Slovakia, by the activities of branches established by German banks, and by the forced liquidation of important Czechoslovak banks. In October 1945 the postwar coalition government, as one of its first measures, had nationalized the commercial and other banks (and the large industrial enterprises), but some banking institutions identified with Czechoslovak national aspirations had subsequently been reestablished. It was in the middle of 1948, after the communist take-over, that the banking and credit system began to be cast in the Soviet mold.

The National Bank, which had been one-third government owned since its creation in 1920 and had not been affected by the earlier measures, was nationalized in 1948. Two years later it was taken over by the newly organized State Bank of Czechoslovakia (Státní Banka Ceskoslovenská), which also absorbed the two remaining banks for short-term credit[1] and the postal savings system. A Soviet-type budget, integrating financial flows of the socialized enterprises with the national budget, was not introduced until 1952. At the beginning of 1959 the State Bank acquired the functions of the Investment Bank, which had been created ten years earlier. For a few years, Czechoslovakia had the unique distinction of having concentrated all banking and financing activities in a single bank, since the others were in process of liquidation and were not undertaking

---

[1] *The Tatra Banka, which had been created as a concession to Slovak nationalism, and the Živnostenskà Banka; the latter was reestablished in 1956, with a branch in London, as a bank for foreign private remittances.*

any new operations. The situation ended with the creation of a foreign trade bank—Obchodni Banka (Commercial Bank)—which commenced operations on January 1, 1965, with all the functions typical of such institutions in the communist countries.

In mid-1965, following the East German example, separate bank offices were created for the industrial associations. The primary aim of these offices is to cooperate closely with their particular industry groups in matters of planning and production, to serve the associations' financial needs, and to supervise local bank branches engaged in routine transactions with the associations' component enterprises. In line with the introduction of economic reforms and changes in the organization of industry, a new bank law was passed in 1965 which gave the State Bank greater authority to exercise financial controls in the socialized sector of the economy and empowered it, in the process of planning and extending credit, to make sure that not only bank credits but also other funds belonging to the state are properly utilized.

On the whole, the credit policies of Czechoslovakia have gone through the stages common to the countries that followed the example of the Soviet Union: first, automatic crediting of enterprises, to avoid disruptions of production after the communist reorganization of the banking system; then introduction of the five principles of socialist credit, with emphasis on securing loans by real assets; and soon thereafter the emergence of preferential treatment for enterprises that perform well.[2] Some steps toward greater flexibility were taken in 1957. The first major change in the credit area, however, occurred with a 1958 reorganization of economic administration, which resulted, among other things, in the creation of the industry associations to replace the intermediate administrative organizations that had hitherto been interposed between individual enterprises and the industry ministries. As compared with their predecessors, the associations have more autonomy for financial planning, are permitted to retain a larger part of profits and depreciation funds, and are allowed to use these resources more flexibly. After 1957 the State Bank shifted from making separate short-term loans for individual categories of inventories and supplies to extending loans for

---

[2] See, for instance, the official textbook by J. Petrivalsky and associates, Peněžni Oběh a Úvěr v ČSSR (Monetary Circulation and Credit in Czechoslovakia), Prague, 1963; also S. Potáč, "Credit Planning in the Czechoslovak Socialist Republic", D.K., March 1964, and D. Butakov, "Some Questions of Crediting the Industry of Czechoslovakia", D.K., January 1965.

broadly defined purposes, with emphasis on credits based on total sales. Such loans had been introduced experimentally in 1955, and by 1959 more than two thirds of all inventories were financed on the "turnover basis". Rigid central control of the wages fund has also been given up.

Under the greater financial flexibility introduced in 1957 (before the reorganization of industry), enterprises were given a voice in determining the amount of their working capital. Though the ultimate decision still lay with the industry ministries, the enterprises were permitted to submit their own estimates of needs for the coming year. For selected enterprises, credit-granting procedures were further simplified in 1961 by combining in a single account loans for inventory purposes and loans against drafts in the process of collection. In 1959, enterprises that performed well were released from all restrictions on their utilization of funds on deposit with the bank, while those that were experiencing only temporary financial difficulties were given greater freedom to use their bank balances, obtaining the right to spend up to 20 (in some cases up to 50) per cent of all sales receipts for any legitimate purpose. Bills became payable in the order of receipt, thus doing away with the complex system of priorities still in force in several countries, including the Soviet Union.

Czechoslovakia was among the first communist countries to make a substantial differentiation in interest rates. Until 1959 the standard short-term charge was 3.6 per cent, and double that rate for overdue credits. Exceptions were made for loans to retail trade establishments and loans against drafts in the process of collection; the charge for both of these was 2 per cent. Interest-free loans were available to finance stocks of spare parts and thus assure proper servicing of equipment sold earlier (it appears that, so long as total production and sales were the key success indicators, there was no incentive to carry such inventories). But on January 1, 1959, the short-term interest rate scale was widened. It now ranges from 0.9 per cent (to carry farm products or imported raw materials) to 5.4 per cent (for financing inventories judged to be in excess of requirements). Even higher rates (5.4 per cent to 7.2 per cent) apply to loans made necessary by poor management, and up to 10.8 per cent is charged on overdue loans; loans to pay taxes may carry a penalty as high as 36 per cent per annum. Within specific limits, local bank office managers have been given some latitude in setting rates.

Under the new policies that began to be introduced in 1957, enterprises have been encouraged to enlarge their own resources. At the same time the extension of bank credit was made more flexible, not only for working capital, but also for certain types of decentralized fixed investment. When the Investment Bank, which had channeled budgetary resources into investment, was absorbed by the State Bank in 1959, the intention was to utilize existing facilities for assessing the prospects for proposed loan-financed investment and controlling the use of credit granted for that purpose. The activities of the State Bank in this area were considerably widened after 1959, when it began to engage actively in the financing of decentralized investment. The bank examines the profitability of the proposed project and makes sure that adequate labor is available and that contracts have been signed to obtain the necessary materials; it may require the guarantee of a higher level organization before it grants a loan.

To encourage capital formation in agriculture, a low rate (1.5 per cent) is charged on long-term loans. A portion of the loan balance of farm cooperatives that meet their production goals is written off each year. This portion was formerly 5 per cent of the cost of the investment, but now it cannot exceed the amount of the amortization payments already made. The cost of this subsidy is borne by the budget, from which the State Bank receives refunds for the full amount of loan reductions granted. Another example of the new "constructive use of credit" is the practice of increasing the loan-financed percentage of the construction cost of farm buildings in proportion to cost economies achieved by having work done by members of the cooperatives.

In 1964, lending for modernization and mechanization was liberalized, the upper limit on the cost of such projects was removed, and the types of projects eligible for bank financing were increased. Despite the various relaxations in the extension of rationalization credits, the proportion of bank credit in the financing of fixed investment has remained negligible, but the introduction of economic reforms in 1966 is bound to increase its importance.

Czechoslovakia's financial planning reflects the distinctive characteristics of its credit arrangements. The credit plan covers both short- and long-term credit and both consumer loans and mortgage loans made by savings banks. "Perspective" plans are prepared for periods of up to five years, with related analysis of prospective sources and uses of funds. In effect, both the annual and the longer run plans have become projections prepared jointly by the State Bank and the Ministry of Finance, with the bank branches serving as an intermediate link to the enterprises and collective farms. Local bank offices review the financial positions of individual enterprises and issue credit commitments to them for purchases of raw materials and other supplies, making sure at the same time that the enterprises have obtained outlets for the finished production. The local offices inform the head office of the loan commitments entered into (and also of loan refusals,

TABLE 9

CREDIT PLAN OF CZECHOSLOVAKIA
Percentages based on amounts outstanding January 1, 1964

Loans	Per cent	Resources	Per cent
Loans secured by real assets	**71.1**	**Capital and reserves**	**2.9**
Inventories	49.0		
Other expenditures	1.6	**Deposits of enterprises**	**17.1**
Settlement credits	14.8	Of which:	
Drafts in process of collection	*14.3*	Current accounts	5.6
Loans to make payments	*0.4*	Investment accounts :	2.3
Other credits	2.7	Social insurance	2.8
To replenish working capital	*2.1*		
For payroll purposes	*0.6*	**Deposits of cooperatives**	**4.5**
Overdue loans	3.0	For investment	1.3
		For current production	3.1
Loans for investment purposes	**16.1**		
Government enterprises	1.7	**Deposits of voluntary organizations**	**2.1**
Cooperatives	14.4		
Of which:		**Deposits of savings banks**	**31.3**
Farm cooperatives	*12.6*		
Housing cooperatives	*1.1*	**Other resources**	
		(Budget, note issue,	
Other uses	**12.8**	balance of payments)	**42.1**
Total	**100.0**	**Total**	**100.0**

Note: Because of rounding, data may not add to totals.
Source: S. Potáč, "Credit Planning in the Czechoslovak Socialist Republic", D.K., March 1964, page 81.

along with the reason), and these reports serve as the basis for preparing the plans. Regional and local offices have considerable latitude in allocating (by industry and individual borrowers) the resources that the head office puts at their disposal under a few broad headings (such as inventory loans and loans for fixed investment). The regional offices operate within overall credit quotas assigned to them, but these quotas can be exceeded with the permission of the head office, which retains a reserve within the credit plan for this purpose. Further flexibility is provided by transferring unused funds between loan categories and offices. The structure of the credit plan is shown in Table 9, along with percentage distributions of loans and resources as of January 1, 1964.

A savings bank system, created in 1952, includes the cooperative savings and loan banks, with a separate regional administration for Slovakia (paralleling similar arrangements in the State Bank). It operates through a network of 118 county offices—one for each county—with additional local branches and a large network of almost 6,000 limited agencies in villages, factories, other places of work, and post offices.

The active business of the savings bank system includes the provision of consumer credit and long-term mortgage loans for home construction and repair. Savings banks are the only source of credit, either short- or long-term, available to independent farmers, but the volume of such loans is negligible, and it has been declining over the years. The inflow of funds into the savings banks continues so large (providing nearly one third of the resources for total credit outstanding at the beginning of 1964) that in October 1965 these banks were authorized to make loans to municipal authorities ("local national committees") for service establishments and tourist facilities. Such loans, with maturities of up to five years, are made strictly on the basis of profitability; the terms are negotiated and, if appropriate, the loan carries the guarantee of the municipal authorities. Loans for similar purposes are made available on comparable terms to voluntary organizations (sports, gardening, and so on).

In 1965, after several years of economic setback (particularly severe in 1962-63), a broad program of economic reforms was initiated. It includes most of the changes in the financing of investment already discussed in Chapter 8, and also makes several operational changes in connection with the reorganization of industry and the new role of the State Bank.[3] As a result, the relations between the bank and its borrowers are now more clearly delineated.

Central administrative authorities will no longer set credit limits for individual branches of industry or enterprises. Instead, they will determine the general objectives of credit policy and leave its implementation to the "credit contract" concluded between the State Bank and the enterprise or association. This document, an apparent imitation of the East German *Kreditvertrag*, is intended to replace the multitude of rules and regulations that formerly guided the relations between

---

[3] *See M. Koudelká, Finance a Úvěr v Nové Soustavě Řízení (Finances and Credit under the New System of Economic Administration), Prague, 1965, in particular pages 57-67. See also the interview with the general manager of the State Bank, Dr. O. Pohl, in* Rudé Právo *(Prague), May 20, 1964 and the special supplement on banking in Hospodářské Noviny, February 11, 1966. Some of the most interesting articles on the recent Czechoslovak economic reforms are listed in the Bibliographical Note, page 166.*

lenders and borrowers. The contract is entered into for a certain period of time: one year for working-capital credit (with an option to renew), and longer periods if the loan is for investment purposes (the length of time varying with the nature of the investment). The credit lines set in these contracts can be exceeded in stipulated circumstances; they are based largely on total sales, rather than on specific needs. An individual enterprise negotiates its credit contract with the local bank office that serves its financial needs, while the management of an association negotiates an industrywide contract with the bank office attached to that particular association. The latter is supposed to provide broad guidelines to the local bank office in regard to the terms and conditions of the contracts negotiated with the individual enterprises in the association. It appears, however, that in the interest of flexibility the guidelines are not intended to be immutable, and that in certain cases noncompliance is tolerated if it results in greater profitability, a faster turnover of inventories, or similar desirable developments.

In contrast to the earlier years, the most recent modifications in Czechoslovakia's banking structure and credit policies are no longer copies of the Soviet prototype. Rather, they seem to have originated within the country or to be based on the experience of neighbors, notably East Germany. As a matter of fact, the new Czechoslovak policies represent a more radical departure from a centrally planned economy than has so far been undertaken by most of the other communist countries.

14. Hungary

The Hungarian banking system has certain distinguishing characteristics. In the field of credit policy, Hungary has pioneered in many of the changes now being embraced by other communist countries. At first, it introduced the standard system, including in the earlier years (1948-49) automatic crediting of enterprises' working-capital needs, but in 1961 Hungary began to introduce modifications intended to reduce centralized direction of credit and to make interest a tool of credit policy and allocation of capital.

The reconstruction of the Hungarian banking system began after the currency reform of 1946, undertaken to cope with the wild postwar inflation. In May

1947, even before the proclamation of the People's Republic, the National Bank and twelve of the largest commercial banks, which, in effect, controlled a large part of the remaining smaller banks, were put under government control. Six months later the entire banking system was nationalized—as in Rumania, the shareholders were paid a compensation, except those who had been German collaborators—and in the following months it was consolidated along the lines followed in the other communist countries. An agricultural bank was in operation in 1953-54 only, but at present there are but three banking institutions: the National Bank (Magyar Nemzeti Bank), the Foreign Trade Bank (established in 1950), and the Investment Bank. The first two have preserved the corporate form, with shareholders—consisting, in both cases, of a variety of government organizations—holding formal meetings and electing their boards of managers. In some respects the National Bank seems to enjoy more prestige and independence than similar institutions in the other countries, though the Council of Ministers retains ultimate control over its activities.

The nationwide savings bank system (the General Savings Bank), which is administered by the Ministry of Finance, was created in 1949 from various elements of the prewar banking system and the postal savings bank. It was enlarged in 1954 by merging into it the network of farm credit cooperatives, and subsequently a system of credit unions was developed in factories and other places of employment, replacing a similar prewar system that was liquidated after the communist take-over. The credit unions act as agencies of the savings bank system, not only accepting deposits but also making short-term (up to four months) consumer loans to members. Credit cooperatives in villages operate similarly, but the bulk of credit to agriculture is provided by the National Bank through short- and long-term loans to cooperative farms. The predominant part of consumer instalment credit, however, is extended by the savings bank system. In 1963, the maximum amount of credit granted to consumers was increased to 80 per cent of the retail price of the item to be purchased, and simultaneously the period of repayment was lengthened from 9-12 months to 18 months.

Credit planning was introduced in 1950-51. Significant moves in the direction of greater flexibility were made as early as 1957, after the suppression of the revolt. Further steps were taken in 1960, when the drawing-up of quarterly credit plans was abandoned, and again in 1961, when large-scale reforms were introduced. The annual national credit plan now reflects a substantial decentralization of responsibility. It is derived through a system of "two-way planning" that involves both the enterprises and the National Bank. The individual enterprises pre-

157

pare estimates of their working-capital needs. The National Bank then aggregates these figures by industry, compares them with projections of its own—which must be consistent with the central authorities' planned increase in output and with related factors, such as anticipated labor productivity and profitability and recent actual production performance—and examines the reasons for any significant discrepancies between the two totals. This system is not expected to result in a complete resolution of any differences that are found. Rather, it is intended to inquire into what caused the grass-roots assessments of needs to differ substantially from those made at the center. As a matter of practical operation, however, the overall credit plan prepared by the National Bank is considered not much more than a guideline, because actual crediting is based largely on delivery contracts. The ratio of borrowed funds to total working capital has increased gradually with the passage of time, and now averages more than 50 per cent in industry.

Each enterprise can use its borrowed funds for any needs arising in connection with its regular activities, in the same way as it uses its own resources. When necessary, such general "production credit", based on production levels and supported by actual sales contracted, is supplemented by "specific-purpose" loans granted by the National Bank on the basis of requests addressed to it by the individual enterprises. The interest charged for these credits depends in each case on their purpose, and ranges between 0.5 per cent, for additional inventories constituted in accordance with government targets, and 6 per cent for excessive inventories of required materials (when measures for orderly liquidation have been taken), with a penalty rate of up to 18 per cent charged for funds needed to carry unwanted inventories. In addition, enterprises that operate at a profit are given credit lines under which they can obtain, without having to produce reasons, thirty-day "liquidity" loans for meeting any temporary needs.

A charge on the use of capital in the form of a tax for the benefit of the budget was introduced as of the beginning of 1964, with the aim of improving the allocation of fixed capital (on which the annual charge is 6 per cent) and reducing the amount of working capital (5 per cent is charged on funds allocated to and "owned" by enterprises). Greater reliance on credit as contrasted with grants for the financing of investment is now being considered.

15. Bulgaria

At the time Bulgaria's industry was nationalized, in December 1947, its private commercial banks were either liquidated or merged with expropriated or newly established government-controlled credit institutions. The Bulgarian National Bank (Blgarska Narodna Banka) was given the functions of the former central bank and the responsibility of extending short-term credits to nationalized industry. It was also directly subordinated to the Council of Ministers. The Investment Bank, formed from the prewar Banque Hypothéquaire Bulgaire (mortgage bank), was placed under the control of the Finance Ministry. Credit cooperatives, "popular banks", and the postal savings system were made subject to the supervision of the National Bank. The cooperatives, operating as mutual societies with membership capital, accepted deposits from the rural population and extended small loans to peasants for bolstering agricultural production, whereas the popular banks served the urban population and provided loans to craftsmen, artisans, and the remaining private entrepreneurs.

A credit reform of 1950-51 further streamlined the banking system in line with concepts and techniques borrowed from the Soviet Union. The popular banks were dissolved, their assets and liabilities going to the National Bank, and the credit cooperatives were transformed into ordinary consumer cooperatives. At the same time, as in Czechoslovakia, a single savings bank, with numerous branches throughout the country, was substituted for the network of postal savings banks.

As a result of these reforms, the functions and organizational arrangements of the Bulgarian National Bank became those of a typical monobank and the Soviet principles of credit extension became the governing rule. The simultaneous introduction of cash and credit planning, which was made its responsibility, considerably tightened the National Bank's control over money and credit and over all financial transactions of state enterprises. It was no longer possible, as it was in 1947-48, for the socialized sector to receive substantial credits solely under the government's guarantee and without collateral. Changes were made also in clearing arrangements. Until 1950, enterprises had not been required to settle all payments through the National Bank, and interunit credit was officially tolerated until 1951. After the reform, all enterprises were compelled to deposit their cash proceeds in bank accounts, and to settle their indebtedness through the National Bank clearing accounts.

As in the other communist countries, short-term loans constitute the bulk of total credits extended, the percentage having risen steadily from 53 in 1948 to

86 in 1958. The simultaneous sharp curtailment of medium- and long-term lending is attributable to a shift from loans to grants, as a result of the credit reform of 1950-51, in financing the investment of nationalized enterprises. The National Bank now provides more than 95 per cent of all short-term credit, the remainder being granted for special purposes by the Investment and Foreign Trade Banks. Although Bulgaria is the least industrialized country in Eastern Europe, the structure of short-term credits extended by its National Bank does not differ significantly from the other communist countries: the trade sector receives more than half and industry only about one third, of which the lion's share goes to the light manufacturing and food industries.

Until 1961, agriculture received only about 3 per cent of the National Bank's total credit extensions, even though farming accounted for about 35 per cent of the national income. A significant portion of seasonal funds was supplied to agriculture by the procurement agencies in the form of advance payments for compulsory deliveries. Credit was extended to collective farms only for certain current production needs, such as the purchase of seed, fertilizer, fuel, and spare parts. In 1961, however, in line with a general monetization of the relationship between the state and agriculture, the National Bank assumed responsibility for providing seasonal farm credit directly. It also took over from the Investment Bank the extension of medium- and long-term credits for fixed investment in agriculture. As a result, the National Bank's provision of short-term credit to collective farms was in 1962 approximately twenty times as large as in 1958. The prerequisite for extending long-term credits to collective farms is that at least 30 per cent of the investment be covered by "own" funds. The charge for these credits is 3 per cent and the maturity between three and ten years, depending on the purpose.

Differentiation of interest rates is still little used. The rates are 2 per cent for the replenishment of working capital (geared to turnover) and 4 per cent for all other credits, including seasonal needs and the procurement of agricultural commodities. Despite continuous efforts to reduce their amount, overdue loans have remained a problem. They represented about one fifth of all credits outstanding in 1956, and by 1960 the proportion was only slightly reduced to about one sixth. One of the measures aimed at reducing the amount of overdue loans empowers the National Bank to place credits extended for the accumulation of unplanned inventories in a "special category", on which the interest rate is raised to 7 per cent. Until recently, however, this sanction was applied quite infrequently.

Loans for small modernization and for the expansion of consumer goods production are used essentially for nonplanned investment with short recoupment periods; they have a maximum duration of two years. In spite of their low cost—2 per cent per annum—they are used sparingly. In 1955 only 40 per cent of all such credits authorized in the plan were used. During the succeeding years the ratio rose, reaching 84 per cent in 1959, but difficulties in obtaining materials and equipment remain an obstacle to this type of investment.

The Investment Bank has certain distinguishing characteristics. In addition to pursuing the usual activities assigned to such banks in Eastern Europe, it is in charge of long-term credit to craftsmen cooperatives and private entrepreneurs as well as to building cooperatives and individuals for residential construction. Prior to 1961, the Investment Bank extended long-term credit to collective farms; this function, however, is now performed by the National Bank. The bulk of the Investment Bank's lending—about three fourths of the total prior to 1960—has been for capital formation by collective farms. It also provides long-term (three to ten years) credits to farmers, at rates ranging from 3.5 per cent to 4 per cent, for purchases of cattle and agricultural implements, for construction of farm facilities, and for the acquisition of seed. Only members of collectives and workers in state-owned agricultural establishments are eligible to receive such loans, and preference is given to farmers who contract with the government for the delivery of agricultural produce.

Also, in contrast to other Investment Banks, that of Bulgaria receives deposits from government enterprises (mainly depreciation reserves), from cooperatives, and from individuals. In making loans to individuals for residential construction, preference is given to those who hold earmarked savings accounts with the bank, and therefore the number of individual depositors has risen rapidly. As a result of this relatively broad field of activity, the Investment Bank—unlike its counterparts in the other countries—has a considerable network of branches.

The State Savings Bank holds about 85 per cent of the population's savings, the remainder being deposited in earmarked accounts with the Investment Bank. Deposits in savings banks increased sharply after 1956, when the virtually mandatory purchase of government bonds was discontinued. As in Rumania the State Savings Bank engages in no lending activities, consumer credit being extended by the retail establishments. Its net inflow of funds constitutes a budget resource.

Before the establishment of the Foreign Trade Bank in February 1964, all foreign exchange and foreign trade credit transactions were carried out by the National Bank, and short-term loans to domestic foreign trade organizations for the importation of machinery and equipment were made by the Investment Bank. The Foreign Trade Bank is organized as a joint-stock company. Its major stockholders are the National Bank and other official institutions and government departments.

Bulgaria was the last of the countries to shift to a new economic policy, though it followed the Soviet Union by only a few months. Nevertheless, its new policies, announced in December 1965, go as far as the most radical innovations introduced anywhere in Eastern Europe. The managements of individual enterprises now have more independence, and their activity is guided by a much reduced number of physical indicators. Contractual relations between enterprises are encouraged, including the right to negotiate certain prices instead of applying prices that are centrally determined. Individual enterprises establish their own working-capital needs, and are able to obtain credit on more flexible terms, including credit for a variety of decentralized investments. Prices paid to producers for export goods are more closely geared to world prices. Moreover, certain firms that produce for export are able to deal directly with their foreign customers, bypassing government export monopolies.

Changes in the financing of investment, capital maintenance, and technological improvement follow the pattern now adopted in other communist countries, notably Poland, with a larger portion of profits retained in order to supply resources for projects carried out on the initiative of the enterprise itself.[1] Bulgaria has borrowed from neighboring Yugoslavia the technique of investment auctions. Centrally planned new projects are allocated to existing enterprises on the basis of competitive bidding. Such enterprises present their cost and profit estimates and indicate the degree to which they are ready to participate in financing the new projects—the remainder to be provided by outright budgetary grants—and ministries and other organizations in charge of investment allocate the projects on the basis of the most advantageous bids received. Bank credit is made available to finance part of the enterprises' share in the cost of such projects.

[1] *For a brief summary, see the economic theses of the Politbureau of the Bulgarian Communist Party in E.G., No. 50 (December 1965), page 40.*

Bibliographical Note

Relatively little is available in English on money and banking in Eastern European countries other than the Soviet Union, and much of that is out of date. Thus for these countries the following bibliography concentrates on primary sources and supplements them with references to monographs and journal articles in Russian. Further bibliographical references on specific issues and recent reforms are to be found in the text footnotes. In addition, the monthly publication of the State Bank of the Soviet Union *(Den'gi i Kredit)* frequently carries articles and short notes on recent developments in other communist countries. Other useful sources include the monthly review of the National Bank of Poland *(Wiadomości Narodowego Banku Polskiego),* the official Ministry of Finance periodicals of the Soviet Union, Poland, and East Germany *(Finansy SSSR, Finanse,* and *Deutsche Finanzwirtschaft,* respectively), and the Czechoslovak monthly periodical *Finance a Úvěr.*

There are various studies in English on money and banking in the Soviet Union, ranging from pioneering theoretical exploration to magazine articles for the general reader. These are readily accessible, however, and no attempt has been made to list them. Of the extensive bibliography in Russian, only the more important and more relevant titles are included. The system of transliteration used in this study is that followed by the United States Library of Congress.

GENERAL

V. Bochkova *et al., Banki i kredit v stranakh narodnoi demokratii* (Banks and Credit in the Countries of People's Democracy), Moscow, 1961.

D. Butakov, "Noncash Settlements in the European Socialist Countries", *Den'gi i Kredit,* September 1964.

Finansovo-Kreditnyi Slovar' (Dictionary of Finance and Credit), 2 vols. Moscow, 1961 and 1964.

L. I. Frei, *Mezhdunarodnye raschety i finansirovanie vneshnei torgovli sotsialisticheskikh stran* (International Settlements and Financing of Foreign Trade of the Socialist Countries), Moscow, 1965.

V. P. Komissarov and A. N. Popov, *Den'gi, kredit i finansy evropeiskikh stran narodnoi demokratii* (Money, Credit, and Finances of the European Countries of People's Democracy), Moscow, 1960.

SOVIET UNION

M. Atlas, *Razvitie Gosudarstvennogo Banka SSSR* (The Development of the State Bank of the USSR), Moscow, 1958.

M. B. Bogachevskii, *Finansy i Kredit SSSR* (Finances and Credit of the USSR), Moscow, 1964.

Gosudarstvennyi Bank SSSR K XXII s'ezdu KPSS (The State Bank of the USSR; Report to the 22nd Congress of the Communist Party of the Soviet Union), Moscow, 1961.

V. V. Ikonnikov, *Kredit v sotsialisticheskom obshchestve* (Credit in the Socialist Society), Moscow, 1959.

G. Menz, *Das sowjetische Bankensystem* (The Soviet Banking System), West Berlin: Duncker & Humbolt, 1963. Contains an extensive bibliography.

V. F. Popov, editor, *Gosudarstvennyi Bank SSSR, 1917-1957* (The State Bank of the USSR, 1917-1957), Moscow, 1957.

Y. E. Shenger, *Ocherki sovetskogo kredita* (Essays on Soviet Credit), Moscow, 1961.

G. Shvarz, *Beznalichnyi Oborot i Kredit v SSSR* (Noncash Turnover and Credit in the USSR), Moscow, 1963.

M. M. Usoskin, *Organizatsiia i planirovanie kredita v SSSR* (The Organization and Planning of Credit in the USSR), Moscow, 1961.

POLAND

S. Bartoszewicz and A. Zwass, "Concerning the Improvement of the Methods of Administering the Industry of the Polish People's Republic", *Voprosy Ekonomiki,* August 1965.

D. Butakov, "New Developments in the Financing of Industry in Poland", *Finansy SSSR,* November 1965.

"The Direction of Changes in the System of Planning and Management of the National Economy", *Polish Reports,* Numbers 8 and 9, 1965.

Finanse Polski Ludowej 1944-1960 (Finances in People's Poland, 1944-1960), Warsaw, 1964.

W. Jaworski, *Zarys rozwoju systemu kredytowego w Polsce Ludowej* (Essay on the Development of the Credit System in Poland), Warsaw, 1958.

J. M. Montias, *Central Planning in Poland* (New Haven: Yale University Press, 1962).

C. Slawinski, "Financing Foreign Trade in Poland", *Quarterly Review* (Moscow Narodny Bank, Ltd., London), Autumn 1964.

RUMANIA

M. Năstase, *Planificarea creditului pe termen scurt în R. P. R.* (Planning of Short-term Credit in the People's Republic of Rumania), Bucharest, 1957.

V. Pîrvu, "Bank Levers Assist in the Development of the National Economy", *Probleme Economice,* June 1965.

A. Vijoli, *Organizatsiia finansirovaniia, kreditovaniia i raschetov v RNR* (Organization of Financing, Crediting, and Payments in the People's Republic of Rumania), Russian translation, Moscow, 1963.

EAST GERMANY

H. Finger, E. Polaschewski, and W. Stoll, *Kredit, Zins und Zahlungen im System ökonomischer Hebel* (Credit, Interest, and Payments in the System of Economic Levers), East Berlin, 1965.

S. Friebe, *Der Kredit in der Zentralverwaltungswirtschaft sowjetischen Typs, unter besonderer Berücksichtigung der Kreditpolitik in der sowjetischen Besatzungszone Deutschlands* (Credit in the Soviet-Type Centrally Planned Economy, with particular consideration of Credit Policy in the Soviet-Occupied Zone of Germany), West Berlin: Duncker & Humbolt, 1957. Contains an extensive bibliography.

D. Hunstock and H. Keller, *Zur Kreditplanung im neuen ökonomischen System* (A Contribution to Credit Planning in the New Economic System), 2nd revised edition, East Berlin, 1965.

G. Moiseenko, "Concerning the New System of Payments in the German Democratic Republic", *Den'gi i Kredit,* July 1965.

N. B. Tsapkin, *Finansy i kredit v Germanskoi demokraticheskoi respublike* (Finances and Credit in the German Democratic Republic), Moscow, 1959.

CZECHOSLOVAKIA

Basic Questions of the Financial Economy of the Czechoslovak Socialist Republic (written by the staffs of the Ministry of Finance and the State Bank of Czechoslovakia, mimeographed), Prague, 1965.

D. Butakov, "Some Questions of Crediting the Industry of Czechoslovakia", *Den'gi i Kredit,* January 1965.

M. Fremer, "The New System of Planned Management of National Economy in Czechoslovakia", *Voprosy Ekonomiki,* November 1965.

K. Kouba, "New System of Management of the Economy of the CSSR", *Mirovaia Ekonomika i Mezhdunarodnye Otnosheniia,* February 1966.

"A Note on Banking in Czechoslovakia", *Quarterly Review* (Moscow Narodny Bank, Ltd., London), Spring 1965.

Politicka Ekonomie, April 1965 (Special issue of the Czechoslovak economic monthly devoted to new economic policy; contains brief English summaries.)

S. Potáč, "Credit Planning in the Czechoslovak Socialist Republic", *Den'gi i Kredit,* March 1964.

S. Potáč, "Financial Levers", *Izvestia,* June 28, 1966.

N. Pusenkov, "The New System of Management and Czechoslovakia's Foreign Trade", *Vneshniaia Torgovlia,* December 1965.

HUNGARY

Z. Atlas, "Methods and Practice of Crediting in Hungary", *Den'gi i Kredit,* February 1962.

I Felvideki and R. Roka, "Crediting Extension and Credit Planning in the Hungarian People's Republic", *Den'gi i Kredit,* April 1964.

BULGARIA

R. Chubriev, "The Structure and Control of the Cash Plan in Bulgaria", *Den'gi i Kredit,* December 1963.

B. Isaev, *Denezhno-kreditnaia sistema Narodnoi Respubliki Bolgarii* (The Monetary and Credit System of the People's Republic of Bulgaria), Moscow, 1956.

"The New System of Planned Guidance", *Ekonomicheskaia Gazeta,* No. 50, December 1965.

I. Nikolov and G. Sotirov, "Short-term Crediting of Agricultural Cooperatives by the Bulgarian National Bank", *Den'gi i Kredit,* May 1964.